EXTRA!
ALL STAR
PIN-UP
INSIDE

topps

BASEBALL
BUBBLE GUM
5¢

FREE! MAGIC MAGNET SET

Now you can put on your own amazing and astound your friends. Here's what you get: 2 magnets, 2 steel balls, wooden dowel and an instruction sheet for performing magic tricks with magnets. Send 25¢ BAZOOKA comics or 25¢ and 5 comics to BAZOOKA MAGNETS or Box 9200, St. Paul, Minn. 55177 Use 443. Comics not transferable. Valid only where legal.
INCLUDE YOUR ZIP CODE

©TOPPS CHEWING GUM, INC., MFR., BROOKLYN, N. Y. MADE & PRINTED IN U.S.A. GUM BASE SUGARS, CORN SYRUP, FLAVOR & U.S. CERTIFIED COLOR CONTENTS: 1 SLAB BUBBLE GUM PLUS PICTURE CARDS

©TOPPS CHEWING GUM, INC., BROOKLYN, N.Y. MADE & PRINTED IN U.S.A. GUM BASE, SUGAR, CORN SYRUP, SOFTENERS NATURAL & ARTIFICIAL FLAVOR, CORN SYRUP, SOFTENERS IN CANADA MADE AND DISTRIBUTED BY O-PEE & ARTIFICIAL COLORS UNDER LICENSE WITH TOPPS CHEWING GUM, INC., LTD., LONDON, ONTARIO CONTENTS: 1 STICK GUM PLUS PICTURE CARDS

Just like the big leaguers wear! Flip-on for sun, flip-back for shade. 2 sizes. Send $.500 Bazooka comics or $1 and 20 Bazooka comics and send to: BAZOOKA SUNGLASSES, Box 30 Brooklyn, N.Y. 11232

3 value FREE! real Baseball Sunglasses

Chew the chew the Champ

THE ATOM Bazo

TOPPS
BASEBALL
PICTURE CARDS
PLUS ⅜ OZ. BUBBLE GUM 5¢

Collect the complete set of
TOPPS GIANT-SIZE BASEBALL CARDS

© 1983 TOPPS CHEWING GUM, INC., MFR., BROOKLYN, N.Y., MADE IN U.S.A., PRINTED IN U.S.A.
GUM BASE, SUGARS, CORN SYRUP, FLAVOR & U.S. CERTIFIED COLOR

Play "WINNING LINE-UP" BASE-ALL GAME
GAME CARD INSIDE
NO PURCHASE NECESSARY TO PLAY

To obtain free game card, write to: GAME CARD, P.O. Box 1006, SYOSSET, N.Y. 11775 Offer ends 12/15/83.

BONUS PRIZE OFFER
Collect game cards totaling 25 Bonus Runs & choose a baseball collector's card and sets. Mail game cards a 50¢ postage & handling to: BONUS, box with game card. Offer ends 12/15/83.

Topps Giant Baseball Picture Cards brings full-color photographs of famous New Big Size! Each card includes the mighty and official lifetime statistical records this 'giant' size, prize collection will be series by every lover of the great Ame
COLLECT THE SET! INSIST ON TOPPS GIANT

J. Clark, K. Her
D. Concepcion, K. Her
SET 8: S. Garvel
E. Murray, Jan
R. Jackson, B. Su
SEE OTHER WRAPS
SETS 1-2, 3-4, 5

TOPPS
BASEBAL

YANKEE GREATS

100 CLASSIC BASEBALL CARDS

Topps 1951 Blue Backs card

YANKEE GREATS

100 CLASSIC BASEBALL CARDS

Bob Woods

Foreword by Dan and David Mantle

Stewart, Tabori & Chang, New York

ACKNOWLEDGMENTS: The author would like to thank the many people at the Topps Company who provided guidance and assistance for this book—including Ira Friedman, Adam Levine, Mark Sapir, Clay Luraschi, and Joe Ribando—and, for their past contributions to other baseball projects, former Topps executives Arthur Shorin and Sy Berger. Thanks also go to Abrams editorial director Jennifer Levesque, who pulled together the many elements of the book, and to her staff, in particular copy editor Maureen Klier, designer Francis Coy and design manager Kara Strubel, production supervisor Jacquie Poirier, and managing editor David Blatty. Thanks to COMC.com trading-card consignment service, for providing some cards. Gratitude also goes to the Mickey Mantle family for their gracious cooperation—as well as to Yankees players past and present who have provided the greatness that inspired this book. Finally, the author would like to thank his wife, Sue, and kids, Max, Emma, and Grace, not only for their love and support but also for sharing in the fun of being Yankees fans.

Editor: Jennifer Levesque
Designer: Francis Coy
Production Supervisor: Jacquie Poirier

Jacket design: Jacob Covey
Case photography: Geoff Spear

Cataloging-in-Publication Data has been applied for and may be obtained from the Library of Congress.

ISBN: 978-0-8109-8838-5

Published in 2012 by Stewart, Tabori & Chang
An imprint of ABRAMS

Printed and bound in Hong Kong, China
10 9 8 7 6 5 4 3 2 1

Stewart, Tabori & Chang books are available at special discounts when purchased in quantity for premiums and promotions as well as fundraising or educational use. Special editions can also be created to specification. For details, contact specialsales@abramsbooks.com or the address below.

ABRAMS
THE ART OF BOOKS SINCE 1949

115 West 18th Street
New York, NY 10011
www.abramsbooks.com

© T.C.G. Printed in U.S.A.

TEAM

97

CARD

NEW YORK YANKEES

Home Field: Yankee Stadium   Seating Capacity: 67,000
R. F. Fence: 296'   L. F. Fence: 301'   C. F. Fence: 461'
Pennant Winning Teams: 1921-23, 26-28, 32, 36-39, 41-43,
47, 49-53, 55-56*
World Championship Teams: 1923, 27-28, 32, 36-39, 41, 43,
47, 49-53, 56*

ALL TIME YANKEE LEADERS

BAT. AV.	Babe Ruth	.393	1923	MOST HITS	Earle Combs	231	1927
RUNS	Babe Ruth	177†	1921	E. R. A.	Spud Chandler	1.64	1943
R.B.I.	Lou Gehrig	184†	1931	W-L PCT.	Lefty Gomez	.839	1934
HOMERS	Babe Ruth	60*	1927	WINS	Jack Chesbro	41*	1904

*MAJOR LEAGUE RECORD   †AMERICAN LEAGUE RECORD

PLAYERS PICTURED ON FRONT

FRONT ROW: Ford, Martin, Hunter, Carroll, Coach Dickey, Coach Crosetti, Mgr. Stengel, Coach Turner, Berra, Noren, Silvera, McDougald. 2nd ROW: Trainer Mauch, Slaughter, Cerv, Jerry Coleman, Skowron, Howard, Turley, Dixon, Wilson, Rip Coleman, Larson. BACK ROW: Sturdivant, Siebern, Carey, Byrne, Grim, Mantle, Bauer, McDermott, Morgan, Kucks, Collins. Batboys: Carr, Loperfido.

The Mick is in the back row, right in the middle, of this 1957 Yankees team card.

STILL ON TOP

BY DAN & DAVID MANTLE

We were young kids when Dad was playing for the Yankees in the 1950s and '60s, but we have wonderful memories of him and Mom packing up the four of us Mantle boys—including our brothers Mickey Jr. and Billy—and driving from our summer home in New Jersey to Yankee Stadium. Naturally, Dad was our favorite, but it was always such a thrill to be around so many great Yankees— Whitey, Hank, Elston, Yogi, Billy and his other teammates—especially during the many World Series they played, and won, together.

Another fond childhood memory is running around Yankee Stadium, although coming from our family home in pigskin-crazed Texas, we actually played more football than baseball on the outfield grass! In the clubhouse before games, while Dad was getting his legs taped and he and the other players were signing baseballs, there were always packs of Topps baseball cards for us kids. We loved ripping open the wax packs and looking for cards of our favorite players— not surprisingly, they were all Yankees—but also chewing wads of the bubble gum that's long-gone but still associated with Topps cards. In between blowing bubbles, we'd make trades with the other kids, then later bring the cards home and, like so many other collectors, stash them in shoe boxes or stick them in the spokes of our bicycles.

Of course, back then none of us knew how valuable some of those Topps baseball cards would eventually become. (And, yes, our Mom threw out our cards, too!) It wasn't until the mid-1980s, long after Dad retired in 1968, that the "bubble-gum-card craze," as he always called it, began bringing us baby boomers and our kids out of the woodwork. While we'd known before then how much Yankees fans adored Dad, in many ways it was the card collectors who made us—and him—realize just how much he still means to them. Who knew that his 1952 Topps card would someday be worth tens of thousands of dollars, or that his other cards would also become such hot commodities?

Dad really enjoyed appearing at baseball card shows—meeting fans, swapping stories about his long home runs with them, signing their cards, taking pictures with them. He was always so amazed, though, that his '52 card was the top one. And that it graces the cover of this book makes us proud, knowing that it remains the cornerstone of the relationship between Topps and the Yankees.

The later years of Dad's life, before he passed away in 1995, was a time of reflection for him. Those card shows had helped him understand what he meant to people, but during his final days, he opened up to the public as a human being, not just a ball player. So while we will always have wonderful memories of our favorite Yankee—many spurred by his bubble-gum cards—we're happy that Dad's whole life is celebrated today.

—Dan and David Mantle

INTRODUCTION

BY BOB WOODS

Right off the bat, I proudly confess to being a lifelong Yankees fan and passionate admirer of the game of baseball. Growing up in the 1950s and '60s, when baseball was indisputably the national pastime and long before 24-hour sports media, I would get my daily dose of scores and news as a neighborhood paperboy. Every morning, my route didn't start until I'd snatched a paper off the top of the stack and flipped to the sports section to see how Mickey Mantle, Whitey Ford, Elston Howard, Bobby Richardson, and my other pinstriped heroes had fared the day before.

An older brother's obsession with Mantle further infected me with Yankee-itis. And because the Bronx Bombers routinely played in the World Series, I'd get to see them on TV—sometimes thanks to the nuns at my Catholic school who would roll a set into the classroom and let us watch them wrap up yet another world championship.

During those formative years, I enthusiastically joined my generation in collecting baseball cards, and Topps was all the rage back then. Interestingly, the company's roots had nothing to do with baseball or any other sports. It all goes back to Brooklyn in 1938, when four brothers—Joe, Phil, Abe, and Ira Shorin—were struggling to keep their family's tobacco-distribution business from going up in smoke in the face of competition. The siblings agreed that a switch to selling tabs of gum at a penny apiece was the solution, in part because they already had a wholesale distribution system in place. Thus Topps Chewing Gum

Inc. was born in a factory at the foot of the Williamsburg Bridge. (It moved to its present Manhattan headquarters in 19TK.) The company's name purportedly came about when the Shorins had earlier acquired a small candy company in Chattanooga and adopted its moniker, Topps, which also connoted being "tops" in their business. After World War II, Topps sweetened its product line by creating Bazooka bubble gum, cleverly wrapped in comics starring the now iconic Bazooka Joe and His Gang—plus a soothsaying fortune!

Baseball cards have been around since the 1880s, and early on were provided as premiums with tobacco products. Goudey Gum and Bowman Gum began issuing annual sets, featuring each team's roster of players season by season, in the 1930s and '40s. Topps got in the baseball card game in 1949 with Hocus Focus Magic Photo cards, 19 of which featured baseball players. In '51, the company released the so-called Red Backs and Blue Backs baseball set, which doubled as a card game. Topps released its first annual baseball card set in 1952, and has been at it every year since. While there's been plenty of competition, today Topps is Major League Baseball's exclusive card company, producing not only a standard set each season but also several special series. (Topps has made football, hockey, and basketball cards, too, but that's a whole other story.)

Topps baseball cards have obviously evolved over the decades, though they've always occupied a unique place in Americana, shared by kids and adults and passed on from generation to generation. Part of that has to do with baseball's permanence in our culture, the ageless adoration of athletes, and the pleasurable pastime of collecting things. Yet Topps cards—even those beyond baseball—have retained an extraordinary attraction, and new sets are eagerly anticipated every year. Topps fans can't wait to see—and critique—the different designs of the cards, front and back, as well as the player photos, the taking of which has been a rite of spring training for Topps photographers for the past 60 years.

Like millions of other kids, all spring and summer I'd ritualistically tear open dozens of wax packs, stuff slabs of bubble gum in my mouth (to the dismay of dentists everywhere, the gum was discontinued in 1992), and thumb through the cards to see which veterans and rookies I could add to my collection—Yankees, of course, being the major targets. While my card collecting waned in high school and college, my love of the Yankees endured, and when I moved to New York in the mid-1970s, just as the team awakened from its decade-long slumber, adult adoration kicked in . . . and has never faded.

All those factors serendipitously merged in 1990, when my career as a freelance writer and editor led me to Topps. Riding the then-cresting card-collecting wave, I was asked to help create *Topps Magazine*, a quarterly publication that for four years brought together coverage of the hobby and baseball's top players. Although the magazine is long gone, I've continued to write about baseball and have maintained a strong working relationship with Topps. So when I got the assignment to author a book called *Yankee Greats*, using Topps cards as the illustrative focus, personal and professional nirvana was achieved.

Identifying a nice round number of 100 great Yankees—players and managers—wasn't difficult, though readers are apt to quibble

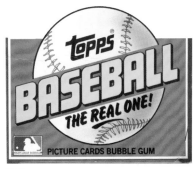

1982 wrapper

with who's been left out. But I worked with a caveat: Only those players pictured on a Topps card could be included. Because Topps didn't start releasing annual sets until 1952, nearly a half century of Yankees greats are not on regular Topps cards. Thankfully, Babe Ruth, Lou Gehrig, Bill Dickey, and other legends have been featured on special Topps cards over the years. But others, including Waite Hoyt, Herb Pennock, Earle Combs, Lefty Gomez, Red Ruffing, Spud Chandler, and Joe Gordon—all Hall of Famers—unfortunately have not. I truly regret not including them here, though I also know that it doesn't diminish their place among the pantheon of superstars who've donned the pinstripes.

Otherwise, choosing which Topps card to include for each player was a subjective process, beyond the requirement that each had to be wearing a Yankees uniform. The market value of the cards—a prime factor among collectors—was not necessarily an issue, though treasured rookie cards are included. In many cases, a player's highlight year or event—Roger Maris in 1961 and Don Larsen in 1956, for instance—was the motivation.

My ultimate hope is that *Yankee Greats* will evoke happy memories, elicit triumphant cheers, and generally celebrate a shared fandom for the most successful and adored team in sports history. It certainly has for me.

Topps Giant Baseball Picture Cards bring you, for the very first time, full-color photographs of famous Big Leaguers . . . in the New Big Size! Each card includes the player's autograph, biography and official, lifetime statistical record. Never offered before, this giant-size, prize collection will be cherished through the years by every lover of the great American pastime.

COLLECT THE SET! INSIST ON TOPPS GIANT-SIZE BASEBALL CARDS!

TOPPS

5¢

BASEBALL

GIANT
SIZE

PICTURE CARDS

PLUS ⁵/₈ OZ.
BUBBLE
GUM

1952 wrapper

PART 1 · 1950s & EARLIER

Just as the greatest Yankee, Babe Ruth, traced his roots to Baltimore, so does the baseball team that he helped make the greatest ever. It all goes back to 1903, when Frank Farrell and Bill Devery purchased the defunct Baltimore Orioles franchise of the American League (unrelated to the current club) for $18,000 and moved it to Manhattan. The team, which played at Hilltop Park, built on one of the borough's highest points, was aptly named the Highlanders. Behind future Hall of Famer Willie Keeler's .313 batting average, Herm McFarland's team-leading five home runs, and fellow Hall of Famer Jack Chesbro's 21–15 pitching line (featuring 33 complete games in 36 starts!), the 1903 Highlanders finished with a fourth-place 72–62 record.

The Highlanders, who first appeared in pinstriped uniforms in 1912, were renamed the Yankees in 1913, the same year they relocated to Manhattan's Polo Grounds, a ballpark they would share with the National League's New York Giants until Yankee Stadium opened in 1923. Colonel Jacob Ruppert and Colonel Tillinghast L'Hommedieu Huston bought the Yankees in 1915 for $1.25 million, and five years later purchased the Babe from the Boston Red Sox for $125,000 and a $350,000 loan against the Fenway Park mortgage.

The Yanks won the AL pennant in 1921 and '22, but both years they were defeated in the World Series by their co-tenants, the Giants. The tables were turned in 1923, when the brand-new House That Ruth Built celebrated the Babe's one-and-only MVP season (go figure!) and eventual slaying of the Giants. Ruth and the rest of the offensive juggernaut known as Murderers' Row powered the 1927 Yankees—considered one of baseball's best teams of all time—to their second

world championship. They repeated in '28, then dominated in the 1930s, with a sweep of the Chicago Cubs in '32 and four straight titles from 1936 to '39.

The Yankees appeared in five World Series in the 1940s and prevailed four times, even as many players left to serve in the military during World War II. Meanwhile Ruth, Lou Gehrig, Tony Lazzeri, and the rest of Murderers' Row were replaced by a new generation of Yankee greats—including Joe DiMaggio, Red Ruffing, Joe Gordon, Charlie Keller, and Joe Page—who would continue the team's winning ways into the 1950s. Then Mickey Mantle, Whitey Ford, Yogi Berra, Vic Raschi, Phil Rizzuto, and a cavalcade of other superstars ran roughshod through the decade, winning six more World Series.

The 1950s, of course, also marks the birth of Topps baseball cards, beginning with the Red Backs and Blue Backs playing-card set in 1951. That was followed by the famous '52 cards, wrapped in colorful wax paper with a slab of bubble gum inside. Many of the familiar features on today's Topps cards—from fully designed fronts to season and career statistics on the backs—were introduced in that first annual set. Other "firsts" followed throughout the '50s, including team logos, cartoons, trivia, action photos, and rookie cards. Bowman Gum competed with Topps in those early years, with the companies vying to sign players to exclusive card contracts. That's why, for example, there were no Topps Mantle cards in 1954 and '55. The battles ceased in 1956, when Topps bought Bowman. Nonetheless, because of the team's success and popularity during that era, to this day Yankees cards from the '50s are revered for both their sentimental and financial value.

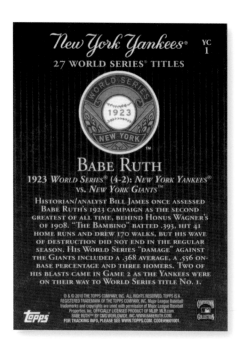

BABE RUTH Incorrigible from an early age, Ruth was sent to St. Mary's Industrial School in his native Baltimore, where he learned reading, writing, and baseball. After six seasons as a dominant left-handed pitcher for the Boston Red Sox, the Babe was sold to the rival Yankees. He transformed himself into the greatest hitter in history and the Yanks into the winningest sports franchise ever. From 1920 to 1931, Ruth led the AL in slugging 11 times, home runs 10 times, walks 9 times, on-base percentage 8 times, and runs 7 times, while 8 times his batting average topped .350. He led New York to its first of 27 (and counting) World Series championships in 1923—remarkably his lone MVP season.

Topps card pictured: 2010 Yankees 27 World Series Titles #1. In 2010, Topps feted the Yanks' 27 championships with a box set featuring a star from each winning team. For players prior to 1951, the 1952 card-front design was resurrected.

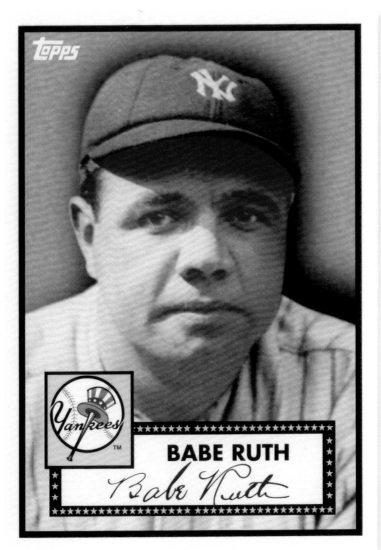

341 | **LOU GEHRIG** First Base

HEIGHT: 6'1"   WEIGHT: 200   BATTED: LEFT   THREW: LEFT
BORN: 6-19-03, NEW YORK, N.Y.   DIED: 6-2-41, NEW YORK, N.Y.

ELECTED TO THE HALL OF FAME IN 1939

COMPLETE MAJOR LEAGUE BATTING RECORD

YEAR	CLUB	G	AB	R	H	2B	3B	HR	RBI	AVG.
1923	YANKEES	13	26	6	11	4	1	1	9	.423
1924	YANKEES	10	12	2	6	1	0	0	6	.500
1925	YANKEES	126	437	73	129	23	10	20	68	.295
1926	YANKEES	155	572	135	179	47	20★	16	107	.313
1927	YANKEES	155	584	149	218	52★	18	47	175★	.373
1928	YANKEES	154	562	139	210	47●	13	27	142●	.374
1929	YANKEES	154	553	127	166	33	9	35	126	.300
1930	YANKEES	154	581	143	220	42	17	41	174★	.379
1931	YANKEES	155	619	163★	211★	31	15	46●	184★	.341
1932	YANKEES	156	596	138	208	42	9	34	151	.349
1933	YANKEES	152	593	138★	198	41	12	32	139	.334
1934	YANKEES	154	579	128	210	40	6	49★	165★	.363★
1935	YANKEES	149	535	125★	176	26	10	30	119	.329
1936	YANKEES	155	579	167★	205	37	7	49★	152	.354
1937	YANKEES	157	569	138	200	37	9	37	159	.351
1938	YANKEES	157	576	115	170	32	6	29	114	.295
1939	YANKEES	8	28	2	4	0	0	0	1	.143
MAJ. LEA. TOTALS:		2164	8001	1888	2721	535	162	493	1991	.340

★LED LEAGUE   ●TIED FOR LEAD

LOU GEHRIG Gehrig's path to greatness began circuitously and ended tragically. He was a star high school player who had grown up as a New York Giants fan, yet Giants manager John McGraw passed on Gehrig, a mistake McGraw's Yankees counterpart, Miller Huggins, avoided. It took a couple of seasons for Gehrig to supplant longtime starter Wally Pipp at first base, but once he did, on June 2, 1925, Gehrig's legendary streak of 2,130 games ensued. Over that period, the Iron Horse won four home run crowns, two MVP awards, and six World Series titles. His career was cut short in 1939 by an incurable, fatal neuromuscular disease that resulted in his death in 1941 and that now bears his name.

Topps card pictured: 1976 #341. The Iron Horse was one of 10 baseball greats, designated by the *Sporting News* as All-Time All-Stars, honored on special cards in the '76 set.

The Sporting News
ALL-TIME ALL-STARS

LOU GEHRIG
1B

TONY LAZZERI On his way up through the minor leagues to becoming a member of the late-1920s Yankees lineup known as Murderers' Row, Lazzeri stung more than a few balls for the Pacific Coast League's Salt Lake City Bees. In 1925, he batted .355 with 252 hits, 52 doubles, 14 triples, 222 RBIs, and 60 home runs—at the time the most ever hit in professional baseball. That offensive outburst triggered a deal that brought him to the Yanks, where his prodigious numbers and skills as a slick second sacker helped propel the team to seven World Series, of which they won five.

Topps card pictured: 2010 Yankees 27 World Series Titles #5. On May 24, 1936, Lazzeri recorded an AL-record 11 RBIs—with a triple and three homers, two of them grand slams—versus the Phillies at Shibe Park.

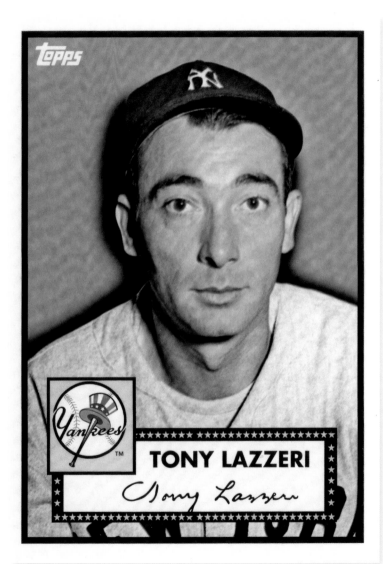

BILL DICKEY "I owe everything I did in baseball to Bill Dickey." That quote from Yogi Berra, a man known for much quirkier ones, speaks volumes about both these Hall of Fame catchers. Dickey played alongside a constellation of superstars—Ruth, Gehrig, DiMaggio—yet put up his own stellar numbers: 11 seasons hitting over .300 and four with 20-plus home runs and 100-plus RBIs. His savvy handling of pitchers helped the team to eight AL pennants and seven World Series championships. Dickey ended his career mentoring Berra, who inherited not only Dickey's prowess but also his number 8, which the Yankees later jointly retired in both men's honor.

Topps card pictured: 1952 #400. Because collectors often secured cards, in numbered order, with rubber bands, a valuable card in the '52 set is Andy Pafko's #1, which endured damaging wear and tear and is scarce.

BILL DICKEY

JOE DiMAGGIO

408

Outfield: New York Yankees® Home: San Francisco, CA
Born: Nov. 25, 1914, Martinez, California
Ht.: 6'2" Wt.: 193 Bats: Right Throws: Right

NOT VALID WITHOUT STICKER

☆ Despite injuries in 1951, the incomparable "Yankee Clipper" still managed to contribute a dozen roundtrippers to bring his total to 361 - currently fifth-most in the game's annals. Clutch as always, Joe knocked home 5 runs in the Yankees six-game World Series win over the Giants. He'll forever be known as a three-time MVP and the man with the 56-game hitting streak in 1941!

MAJOR LEAGUE BATTING RECORDS   FIELDING RECORDS

	Games	At Bat	Runs	Hits	Home Runs	RBI	Batting Average	Put-outs	Assists	Errors	Field. Avg.
PAST-YEAR	116	415	72	209	12	71	.263	288	11	3	.990
LIFE-TIME	1736	6821	1390	2214	361	1537	.325	4529	153	105	.978

JOE DiMAGGIO Before he married (and within a year divorced) Marilyn Monroe, and long before Paul Simon wondered where he'd gone, Joltin' Joe enjoyed a long, highly visible love affair with Yankees fans. His consistent productivity is legendary: Over 13 seasons in pinstripes, the Yankee Clipper gracefully defended center field while clobbering 361 homers, averaging 118 RBIs, and compiling a .325 batting average. He won three MVP awards, two batting titles, and nine World Series rings. In 1941 the collective baseball nation turned its eyes to DiMaggio's immortal 56-game hitting streak, during which he amassed 91 hits in 223 at-bats, averaging .409.

Topps card pictured: 2007 "Cards That Never Were" #408. In 2007, Topps issued retro cards of DiMaggio and Ted Williams in 1952 designs.

JOE DiMAGGIO

PHIL RIZZUTO The Scooter remains one of the most beloved players—and broadcasters—in Yankees history. The Hall of Fame shortstop was appreciated for his "scootability" to get after balls; he finished in the top three in fielding percentage eight times. His quick bat and speed on the base paths made him a small-ball wizard; he led the AL in sacrifice bunts four straight seasons (1949–1952). Rizzuto put it all together in 1950, winning the MVP Award and his fourth of seven World Series rings. During his four decades in the Yankees broadcast booth, "Holy cow!" followed great moments, while players were routinely called "huckleberries."

Topps card pictured: 1952 #11. Cards from the '52 set measured 2⅝ by 3¾ inches. At the time, they were the biggest cards ever produced for over-the-counter sale.

PHIL RIZZUTO

YOGI BERRA Get beyond the Yogi-isms ("It's like déjà vu all over again," "I never said most of the things I said") and the fact that he wore "the tools of ignorance" (catcher's gear), and Yogi is revealed as one of baseball's most brilliant players ever. Behind the plate, he was the solid battery mate for a pantheon of pitchers who hurled the Yanks to 14 AL pennants and 10 World Series titles, and was in the top four in nailing base runners 10 times. At the plate, Yogi's ability to hit almost any pitch and drive in runs earned him three MVP awards and ultimately enshrinement in Cooperstown.

Topps card pictured: 1952 #191. Former Topps executive Sy Berger said that he dreamed up the design for the fabled 1952 set at his kitchen table in Brooklyn.

YOGI BERRA

Yogi Berra

ALLIE REYNOLDS Reynolds achieved greatness throughout his Yankees career—a 131–60 record, a 3.30 ERA, 96 complete games, 27 shutouts, even 41 saves, plus a 7–2 record in six World Series victories—but his 1951 season remains magical. On July 12 he no-hit his original team, the Indians. His bid for a second no-no, on September 28 versus the hot-hitting Red Sox, was in jeopardy as he faced the potentially last batter, Ted Williams. Ahead 0–2, the Splendid Splinter popped up behind home plate, but Yogi Berra dropped the ball. Williams skied another pop up, Yogi snared it, and Reynolds became the first AL pitcher with two no-hitters in a season.

Topps card pictured: 1952 #67. Because baseball cards weren't considered valuable in '52, Topps infamously disposed of unsold boxes by dumping them into the ocean off New Jersey.

ALLIE REYNOLDS

EDMUND WALTER LOPAT *pitcher* **NEW YORK YANKEES**

TOPPS
5

Ht.: 5' 10"
Weight: 182
Throws Left
Bats Left
Home: Hillsdale, N. J.
Born: June 12, 1918

Ed was the top hurler in the A.L. last year chalking up the best Earned Run and Won-Lost Averages! His tantalizing curves and pin-point control permitted the fewest walks and least defeats. When Ed beat the Dodgers in the '53 Series it was his 4th win in 7 Fall Classic Games. Ed had a 21-9 record in 1951.

MAJOR LEAGUE PITCHING RECORD

	Games	Innings	Won	Lost	Pct.	Hits	Runs	E. R.	S. O.	Walks	E. R. A.
Year	25	178	16	4	.800	169	58	48	50	32	2.43
Life	288	2133	147	96	.605	2117	865	743	771	592	3.14

INSIDE BASEBALL

Ed wanted to be a Yank 1st sacker in '36 — but they had Gehrig!

So he tried out and was signed by a Dodger farm. He then became a pitcher.

12 years later he was a Yankee—one of their star chuckers! Ed's won 97 games for them since '48.

© T.C.G. Printed in U.S.A.

EDDIE LOPAT The late broadcaster Mel Allen called him Steady Eddie, which aptly describes Lopat's place on the Yankees pitching staff that won five World Series in a row. Converted from first baseman to left-handed pitcher in the minors, Lopat was a double-digit winner in each of his four years with a mediocre White Sox team before being traded to the Yanks in 1948. From 1949 to '53 he remained a consistent winner, going 80–36 over 1,014 innings with a 2.97 ERA. None other than Ted Williams, one of the greatest hitters ever, ranked Lopat number 1 when naming the five toughest pitchers he'd faced.

Topps card pictured: 1954 #5. None of Lopat's Topps cards feature his actual last name, Lopatynski, which he shortened after making it to the minors so it would fit more easily into a box score.

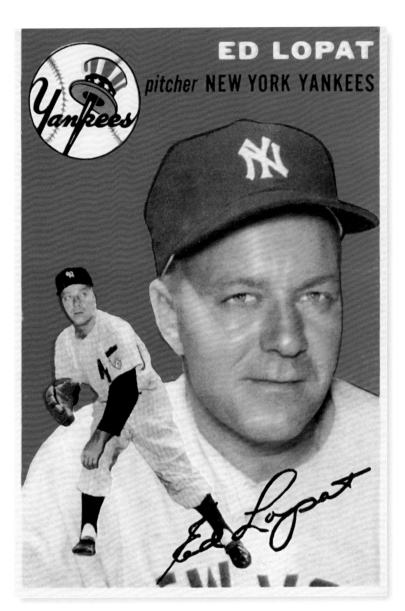

ED LOPAT

pitcher NEW YORK YANKEES

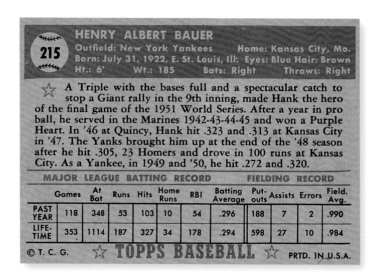

HANK BAUER The burly 6-foot, 202-pound Bauer epitomized the term "tough guy." He grew up admiring the Cardinals' rough-and-tumble Gas House Gang and brought that style of play when he donned the pinstripes in 1948. "It's no fun playing if you don't make somebody else unhappy," Bauer once said. "I do everything hard." He surely hit and threw the ball hard, clobbering 158 homers for the Yanks while averaging .277. With his cannon of an arm, he racked up 88 assists from right field. Playing in nine World Series, seven of them Yankees victories, Bauer produced a record 17-game hitting streak (1956–1958).

Topps card pictured: 1952 #215. Topps 1952 baseball cards were the first to feature official team logos on the front.

HANK BAUER

Hank Bauer

GENE WOODLING Woodling was an integral member of the Yankees dynasty that won an unprecedented five straight World Series from 1949 to '53. Overshadowed by big-name teammates—DiMaggio, Berra, Mantle—he was a reliable left fielder and a steady batsman. Woodling hit .285 over six seasons with the Yanks, topping .300 twice, with a terrific on-base percentage (.388). The lefty hitter proved especially productive in World Series play, twice batting .400 or better and batting .318 overall. Woodling retired in 1962, following a stint with the inaugural Mets, then served as a coach for the Orioles and a scout for the Yankees and Indians.

Topps card pictured: 1952 #99. Bowman also released a baseball card set in 1952 and remained a main competitor—until 1956, when Topps bought Bowman.

GENE WOODLING

GERALD FRANCIS COLEMAN

237

Second Base: New York Yankees Home: San Mateo, Calif.
Born: Sept. 14, 1924, San Jose, Calif. Eyes: Brown
Ht.: 6' Wt.: 170 Hair: Black Bats: Right Throws: Right

☆ Recalled to active duty as a Marine Pilot in May, 1952, Jerry put in 3 years of Service in World War II. He had a year of minor league ball under his belt when he came out of Service and spent 1946 at Bin'ghamton. With Kansas City in '47 and Newark in '48, Jerry joined the Yanks in 1949. In his first year of Big League ball, he hit .275, led all American League Second Basemen in Fielding and was named "Rookie of the Year." A great "clutch" player, he hit .287 in 1950.

MAJOR LEAGUE BATTING RECORD							**FIELDING RECORD**				
	Games	At Bat	Runs	Hits	Home Runs	RBI	Batting Average	Put-outs	Assists	Errors	Field. Avg.
PAST YEAR	121	362	48	90	3	43	.249	272	295	18	.969
LIFE-TIME	403	1331	171	363	11	154	.273	964	1016	50	.975

© T. C. G. ☆ **TOPPS BASEBALL** ☆ PRTD. IN U.S.A.

JERRY COLEMAN Once Coleman finally arrived at Yankee Stadium in 1949, he was battle-tested. He had signed with the Yanks as a 17-year-old in 1942 and hit .304 in the minors. Coleman joined the Navy later that year, earned his wings, then transferred to the Marines. As a bomber pilot, he flew 57 missions in World War II's Pacific theater. He landed back in the Bronx just in time to join the Yankees dynasty that won its first of five straight World Championships. An All-Star and Series MVP in 1950, Coleman missed most of 1952 and '53, returning to the military during the Korean War.

Topps card pictured: 1952 #237. The backs of the 1952 cards included players' 1951 stats but labeled them "Past Year," reportedly so Topps could, if the set sold poorly, market it again in 1953.

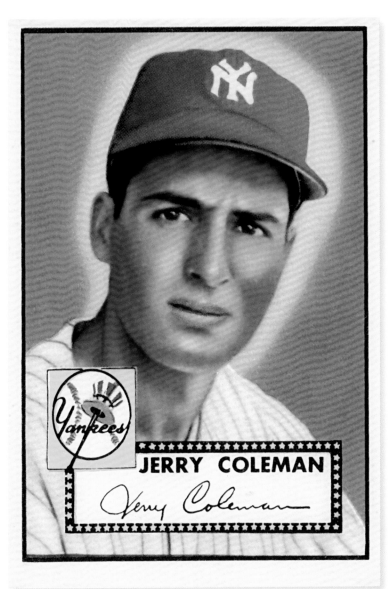

JERRY COLEMAN

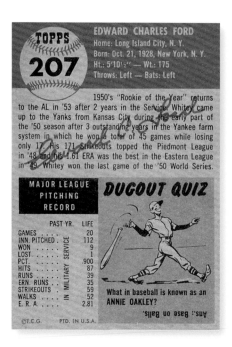

WHITEY FORD   Cy Young lost more games (316) than Whitey Ford won over their respective Hall of Fame careers, which proves the relative value of baseball statistics. To skew the numbers another way, consider that Young, the winningest pitcher ever (511) and namesake of the annual best-pitcher awards, had one World Series title while Ford owns six rings. What's most remarkable about Ford, a.k.a. the Chairman of the Board, is his phenomenal .690 career winning percentage—the highest of any 20th-century pitcher with 200-plus decisions—exemplified by his 25–4 record in 1961, when the southpaw captured his lone Cy Young Award and fifth of those diamond rings.

Topps card pictured: 1953 #207. Whitey's portrait on his 1953 Topps card is one of hundreds of small color paintings of players, based on black-and-white photos, created for the set.

WHITEY FORD

pitcher NEW YORK YANKEES

	Games	At Bat	Runs	Hits	2b	3b	H.R.	R.B.I.	B.Avg.	P.O.	Assists	Errors	F.Avg.
Year	141	533	79	152	10	8	13	53	.285	367	382	13	.983
Life	691	2425	364	677	98	26	60	325	.279	1184	1621	76	.974

GIL McDOUGALD   While a Yankees rookie named Mantle struggled in 1951, another newcomer fared just fine. That was McDougald, whose .306 batting average, 14 homers, and 63 RBIs paced him to AL Rookie of the Year honors. The Mick, of course, would go on to superstardom, yet McDougald continued for nine more seasons as a versatile infielder and a solid hitter. A five-time All-Star, he joined Pete Rose as the only players to be selected for the Mid-summer Classic at three different positions. He also made history in his first of eight World Series, in 1951, becoming only the third player to hit a grand slam.

Topps card pictured: 1956 #225. After buying archrival Bowman during the offseason, Topps was the lone baseball card maker in 1956.

GIL McDOUGALD

2nd-3rd base N.Y. YANKEES

MICKEY MANTLE The Mick was 19 when he burst onto New York's booming baseball scene in 1951 and quickly developed into one of the game's most-feared sluggers and the greatest switch-hitter ever. The Commerce Comet (his nickname at Commerce High School in Oklahoma) was revered not only for launching tape-measure home runs—his 565-foot moonshot at Washington's Griffith Stadium remains the longest on record—but also for his blinding speed on the base paths. He led the American League in homers four times, won three MVP awards, and hit a record 18 round-trippers in 12 World Series. Number 7 was off the charts, though, in his 1956 Triple Crown season: a .353 batting average, 130 RBIs, and 52 home runs.

Topps card pictured: 1952 #311. The gem of Topps' premier baseball card set, Mantle's rookie card has reportedly sold for as much as $250,000.

TOPPS
239

WILLIAM JOSEPH SKOWRON *1st base* **NEW YORK YANKEES**

Height: 6' 1"
Weight: 195
Bats Right
Throws Right
Home: Austin, Minnesota
Born: December 30, 1928

Bill's .318 Batting Average at Kansas City in 1953 was the lowest in his 3 pro seasons, chiefly because of an ankle injury. The previous season at K. C., he was named Minor League Player-of-the-Year after hitting .341 and leading the circuit in Homers (31), RBI's (134) and Total Bases (344). At Norfolk in '52 he topped the Piedmont Loop in Batting with .334.

MINOR LEAGUE BATTING RECORD									FIELDING RECORD			
	Games	At Bat	Runs	Hits	Doubles	Triples	H. R.	R.B.I.	B. Avg.	P. O.	Assists	Errors	F. Avg.
*Year	134	512	72	163	31	12	15	89	.318	1179	61	10	.992
Life	376	1392	257	461	78	32	64	301	.331	1595	76	27	.984

*Record with Kansas City (American Association).

INSIDE BASEBALL

Bill was a baseball, football and basketball star at Purdue!

He was rated one of the top punters in the Big 10 Conference!

A weak fielder at first, he improved his game by attending a Yankee baseball school in the off-season!

©T.C.G. Printed in U.S.A.

MOOSE SKOWRON Moose—Skowron's childhood nickname, a shortening of Mussolini, whom friends said he resembled after he got a buzz cut—was a central figure on the great Yankees teams that played in seven World Series from 1955 to '62, and were victors in four. After batting over .300 his first three seasons, the slick-fielding first baseman made his first All-Star appearance in 1957, finishing the year at .304 with 17 homers and 88 RBIs. He returned to the Midsummer Classic the following four seasons, too. During the Bronx Bombers' mythical 1961 campaign, Moose was one of six Yankees to hit 20 or more round-trippers.

Topps card pictured: 1954 #239. Topps and Bowman battled to sign players to exclusive contracts, so although the '54 Topps set is without Mantle, Stan Musial, and other stars, Ted Williams is pictured on two cards, #1 and #250.

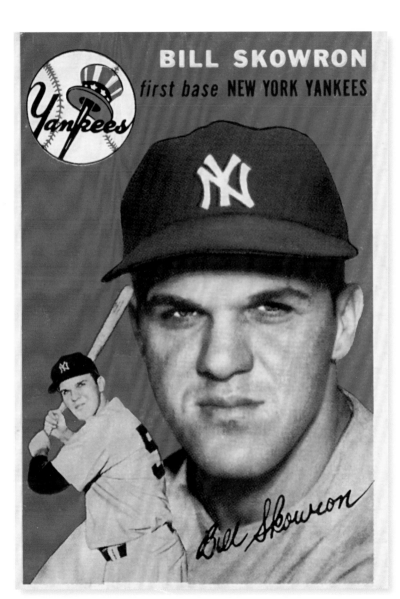

BILL SKOWRON

first base NEW YORK YANKEES

Bill Skowron

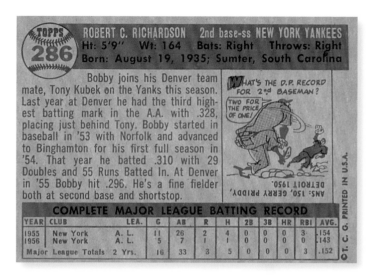

ROBERT C. RICHARDSON 2nd base-ss NEW YORK YANKEES
Ht: 5'9"   Wt: 164   Bats: Right   Throws: Right
Born: August 19, 1935; Sumter, South Carolina

Bobby joins his Denver team mate, Tony Kubek on the Yanks this season. Last year at Denver he had the third highest batting mark in the A.A. with .328, placing just behind Tony. Bobby started in baseball in '53 with Norfolk and advanced to Binghamton for his first full season in '54. That year he batted .310 with 29 Doubles and 55 Runs Batted In. At Denver in '55 Bobby hit .296. He's a fine fielder both at second base and shortstop.

WHAT'S THE D.P. RECORD FOR 2nd BASEMAN?

TWO FOR THE PRICE OF ONE!

ANS: 150, GERRY PRIDDY, DETROIT 1950.

© T. C. G. PRINTED IN U.S.A.

COMPLETE MAJOR LEAGUE BATTING RECORD

YEAR	CLUB	LEA.	G	AB	R	H	2B	3B	HR	RBI	AVG.
1955	New York	A. L.	11	26	2	4	0	0	0	3	.154
1956	New York	A. L.	5	7	1	1	0	0	0	0	.143
Major League Totals 2 Yrs.			16	33	3	5	0	0	0	3	.152

BOBBY RICHARDSON Richardson signed with the Yankees the day he graduated from high school in 1953, a smart move for both parties. The sure-handed second baseman was just 19 when he made his big-league debut in August 1955 and got his first hit off future Hall of Famer Jim Bunning—he still considers that the "game of his life." He joined the team full-time in '57, a year that also marked the first of Richardson's eight All-Star seasons and seven trips to the World Series, where his offensive skills shined brightest. A career .266 hitter in the regular season, he batted .305 in 36 Series games, with a .405 slugging average.

Topps card pictured: 1957 #286. Beginning in 1957, Topps reduced the card size to 2½ inches by 3½ inches, still the standard measure today.

BOBBY **Richardson**

N. Y. YANKEES 2nd B.-S.S.

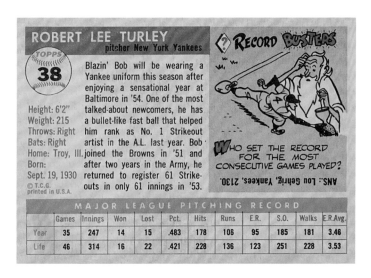

ROBERT LEE TURLEY
pitcher New York Yankees

TOPPS
38

Height: 6'2"
Weight: 215
Throws: Right
Bats: Right
Home: Troy, Ill.
Born:
Sept. 19, 1930
© T.C.G.
printed in U.S.A.

Blazin' Bob will be wearing a Yankee uniform this season after enjoying a sensational year at Baltimore in '54. One of the most talked-about newcomers, he has a bullet-like fast ball that helped him rank as No. 1 Strikeout artist in the A.L. last year. Bob joined the Browns in '51 and after two years in the Army, he returned to register 61 Strikeouts in only 61 innings in '53.

RECORD BUSTERS

WHO SET THE RECORD FOR THE MOST CONSECUTIVE GAMES PLAYED?

ANS.: Lou Gehrig, Yankees, 2130.

MAJOR LEAGUE PITCHING RECORD

	Games	Innings	Won	Lost	Pct.	Hits	Runs	E.R.	S.O.	Walks	E.R.Avg.
Year	35	247	14	15	.483	178	106	95	185	181	3.46
Life	46	314	16	22	.421	228	136	123	251	228	3.53

BOB TURLEY Turley was part of an 18-player trade that landed him in the Bronx in 1955. In his first season with the Yankees, Bullet Bob used an explosive fastball to compile a 17–13 mark, was an All-Star, and pitched in his first of five World Series. In 1958, his best season by far, Turley walked an AL-high 128 batters, but worked out of enough jams to post a 21–7 record, lead the league with 19 complete games, and win the Cy Young Award. In the World Series, his shutout in Game 5 and six-plus innings of relief in Game 7 earned him a championship ring and the Series MVP Award.

Topps card pictured: 1955 #38. In an odd fallout of its contract wars with Bowman, Topps didn't have a licensing agreement with the Washington Senators for the 1955 cards at press time, so the team's cards are labeled "Washington Nationals."

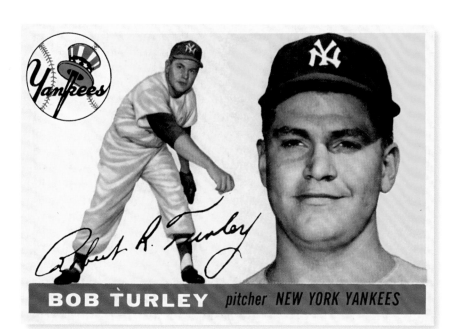

BOB TURLEY *pitcher* NEW YORK YANKEES

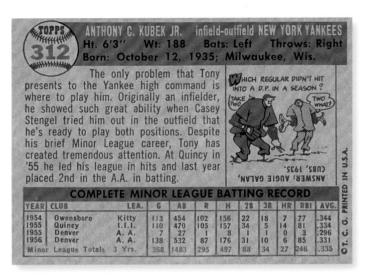

TOPPS 312

ANTHONY C. KUBEK JR.   infield-outfield NEW YORK YANKEES
Ht. 6'3"   Wt: 188   Bats: Left   Throws: Right
Born: October 12, 1935; Milwaukee, Wis.

The only problem that Tony presents to the Yankee high command is where to play him. Originally an infielder, he showed such great ability when Casey Stengel tried him out in the outfield that he's ready to play both positions. Despite his brief Minor League career, Tony has created tremendous attention. At Quincy in '55 he led his league in hits and last year placed 2nd in the A.A. in batting.

WHICH REGULAR DIDN'T HIT INTO A D.P. IN A SEASON?
TAKE TWO
TWO WHAT?

ANSWER: AUGIE GALAN, CUBS, 1935.

O. T. C. G. PRINTED IN U.S.A.

COMPLETE MINOR LEAGUE BATTING RECORD

YEAR	CLUB	LEA.	G	AB	R	H	2B	3B	HR	RBI	AVG.
1954	Owensboro	Kitty	113	454	102	156	22	18	7	77	.344
1955	Quincy	I.I.I.	110	470	105	157	34	5	14	81	.334
1955	Denver	A. A.	7	27	1	8	1	1	0	3	.296
1956	Denver	A. A.	138	532	87	176	31	10	6	85	.331
Minor League Totals 3 Yrs.			368	1483	295	497	88	34	27	246	.335

TONY KUBEK Kubek's memorable Yankees career got off to an auspicious start. Although he played all over the place in 1957—second, third, short, and all three outfield positions—the 21-year-old's versatility and .297 batting average earned him AL Rookie of the Year honors and a trip to the World Series versus the Milwaukee Braves. In Game 3, played in his hometown, in front of friends and family, he socked a surprising pair of homers—considering he'd hit only three during the season. Eventually locked in at shortstop, Kubek would play in five more World Series before retiring to a distinguished career as a broadcaster.

Topps card pictured: 1957 #312. Aside from Kubek's, other prime rookie cards in the 1957 set include future Hall of Famers Don Drysdale (#18), Bill Mazeroski (#24), Whitey Herzog (#29), Frank Robinson (#35), Brooks Robinson (#328), and Jim Bunning (#338).

TONY Kubek
N. Y. YANKEES OUTFIELD

TOPPS

BASEBALL

BUBBLE GUM 5¢

1963 wrapper

PART 2 · 1960s

The 1960s was a half-full, half-empty decade for the Bronx Bombers. It began with another trip to the Fall Classic, thanks in part to a combined 79 home runs belted by Mickey Mantle and his new teammate Roger Maris, who'd been acquired from Kansas City. The Series, against the Pirates, went to seven games, with the Yankees coming out on the losing end. In the bottom of the ninth of Game 7, with the score tied at 9, Bill Mazeroski clouted Ralph Terry's second pitch over the left-field wall at Forbes Field to give the Bucs their first World Series win since 1925.

The M&M Boys staged a much ballyhooed home run derby in '61, dueling all summer to break Babe Ruth's single-season record of 60 homers, set in 1927. An injury took Mantle out of the race in September, with 54 dingers, while Maris stayed strong, finally hitting number 61 on the final day of the regular season. Behind Cy Young winner Whitey Ford, Maris and the rest of the Bombers went on to win their 19th world championship in five games against the Cincinnati Reds.

The Yanks' second-half surge in the 1962 season propelled them to what would be their last World Series victory for the next 15 years—a seven-game thriller against the now San Francisco Giants. They made it to the Series in 1963 and '64 but lost to the Dodgers and Cardinals, respectively. A combination of aging stars, league expansion, and improved competition rendered the Yankees to also-ran status through the rest of the 1960s; they finished above .500 only once, going 83–79 in 1968. Even through the tough times, however, fan favorites such as Elston Howard, Mel Stottlemyre, and Joe Pepitone kept hopes alive.

Topps cards kept the connection between the Yankees and their faithful going, too. Collectors eagerly awaited each season's new designs, as well as cards for the latest crop of up-and-coming rookies, such as Phil Niekro ('64), Jim "Catfish" Hunter ('65), and Reggie Jackson ('69)—all three of whom would someday don the pinstripes and be enshrined in the Hall of Fame. Sets kept growing in number (peaking at 664 in 1969) and in new features, with cards picturing World Series teams, coaches, and league leaders.

TOPPS **60** **ELSTON HOWARD**
Catcher N.Y. Yankees
HT: 6:02 WT: 2ʋ4 BATS: Right
THROWS: Right BORN: 2/23/1929
HOME: Teaneck, N. J.

During the '60 World Series, Elston tied a mark by cracking out two hits in one inning.

ELSTON HAS HIT 5 WORLD SERIES HOME RUNS.

COMPLETE MAJOR AND MINOR LEAGUE BATTING RECORD

YEAR	TEAM	LEA.	G	AB	R	H	2B	3B	HR	RBI	AVG.
1950	Muskegon	Cent.	54	184	22	52	6	2	9	42	.283
1951-2						IN MILITARY SERVICE					
1953	Kansas City	A. A.	139	497	58	142	22	9	10	70	.286
1954	Toronto	Int.	138	497	78	164	21	16	22	109	.330
1955	New York	A. L.	97	279	33	81	8	7	10	43	.290
1956	New York	A. L.	98	290	35	76	8	3	5	34	.262
1957	New York	A. L.	110	356	33	90	13	4	8	44	.253
1958	New York	A. L.	103	376	45	118	19	5	11	66	.314
1959	New York	A. L.	125	443	59	121	24	6	18	73	.273
1960	New York	A. L.	107	323	29	79	11	3	6	39	.245
1961	New York	A. L.	129	446	64	155	17	5	21	77	.348
1962	New York	A. L.	136	494	63	138	23	5	21	91	.279
Major League Totals		8 Yrs.	905	3007	361	858	123	38	100	467	.285

©T.C.G. PRINTED IN U.S.A.

ELSTON HOWARD In 1955, eight years after Jackie Robinson broke baseball's color barrier, Howard became the Yankees' first African American player. He was with the Negro Leagues' Kansas City Monarchs before signing with New York in 1950 and moving up through the farm system. Howard played mostly in the outfield before replacing Yogi Berra as catcher in 1960, when he made his fourth of nine straight All-Star teams. Following a breakout year in 1961 (a .348 batting average, 21 home runs, 77 RBIs) and a solid '62 season, his career-high 28 homers and Gold Glove defense paced Howard to become the first black player to win the AL MVP Award in '63. After retiring, he became the Yanks' first black coach.

Topps card pictured: 1963 #60. Players delighted in messing with Topps photographers. In '63, future broadcaster and funnyman Bob Uecker, then a catcher and right-handed batter for the Milwaukee Braves, posed as a left-hander for his card (#126).

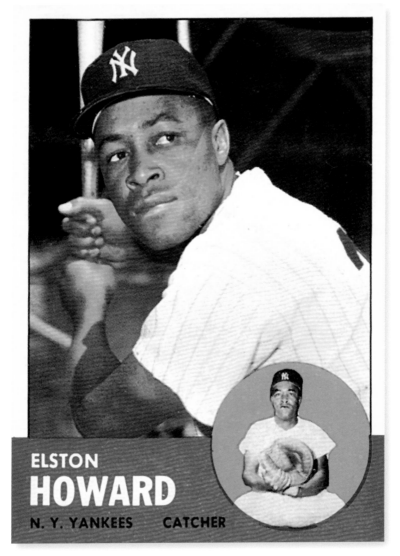

ELSTON
HOWARD
N. Y. YANKEES   CATCHER

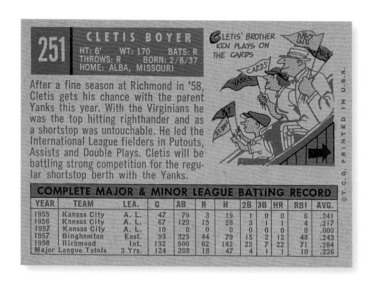

YEAR	TEAM	LEA.	G	AB	R	H	2B	3B	HR	RBI	AVG.
1955	Kansas City	A. L.	47	79	3	19	1	0	0	6	.241
1956	Kansas City	A. L.	67	129	15	28	3	1	1	4	.217
1957	Kansas City	A. L.	10	0	0	0	0	0	0	0	.000
1957	Binghamton	East.	93	325	44	79	15	2	12	48	.243
1958	Richmond	Int.	132	500	82	142	25	7	22	71	.284
Major League Totals		3 Yrs.	124	208	18	47	4	1	1	10	.226

CLETE BOYER Boyer was a steady hitter with decent power in his eight seasons with the Yankees, but at third base he was an absolute wizard, boasting tremendous range and a superb throwing arm. His overall skills—as well as those of superstar teammates Mantle, Maris, Berra, and Ford—helped propel the Yanks to five straight World Series from 1960 to '64 and a pair of championships. In the '64 Fall Classic against the Cardinals, for whom his brother Ken also played at the hot corner (another brother, Cloyd, pitched for St. Louis from 1949 to '52), both Clete and Ken homered in Game 7, which the Cards won.

Topps card pictured: 1964 #251. The '64 set includes an "In Memoriam" card for Ken Hubbs (#550), a rising 22-year-old star for the Cubs when he was killed in a plane crash on February 13, 1964.

cletis boyer

Cletis Boyer

NEW YORK YANKEES
INFIELD

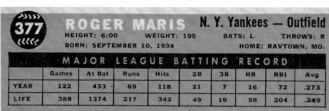

377 ROGER MARIS — N. Y. Yankees — Outfield

HEIGHT: 6:00 WEIGHT: 195 BATS: L THROWS: R
BORN: SEPTEMBER 10, 1934 HOME: RAVTOWN, MO.

MAJOR LEAGUE BATTING RECORD

	Games	At Bat	Runs	Hits	2B	3B	HR	RBI	Avg
YEAR	122	433	69	118	21	7	16	72	.273
LIFE	388	1374	217	342	49	16	58	204	.249

SEASON'S HIGHLIGHTS

- MAY 10: Has 2 HRs, 5 RBIs vs. Det.
- JUNE 22: After being out for 30 days Rog hits 2 doubles vs. Yanks.
- JULY 11: Drives in 3 runs against Chisox.
- JULY 23: Hits HR, double and single against Orioles.
- JULY 27: Blasts grand slam homer to beat Washington 7-6.
- DEC. 13. Rog is traded to Yanks.

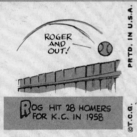

ROG HIT 28 HOMERS FOR K.C. IN 1958

ROGER MARIS After four solid seasons in the majors—two each with the Indians and Athletics—Maris was traded to the Yankees, where he would rise to baseball immortality. The lefty-hitting slugger socked a pair of homers in his very first game, setting the tone for what would be the first of back-to-back MVP titles and establishing Maris's penchant for going deep. His 1961 season remains one for the ages, with Maris and Mantle—the M&M Boys—dueling to eclipse Babe Ruth's single-season home run record of 60. Under intense media scrutiny, Maris prevailed, launching number 61 on the last day of the season.

Topps card pictured: 1960 #377. Maris was featured on another card in the 1960 set (#565), headlined "Sport Magazine '60 All-Star Selection." He finished his first season with the Yankees as the 1960 AL MVP.

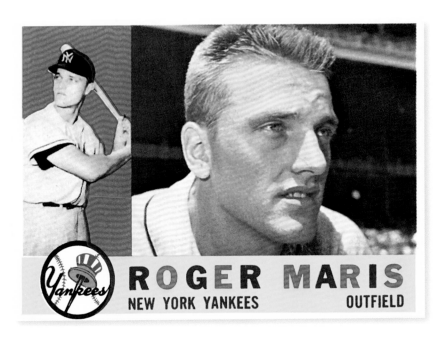

ROGER MARIS

NEW YORK YANKEES OUTFIELD

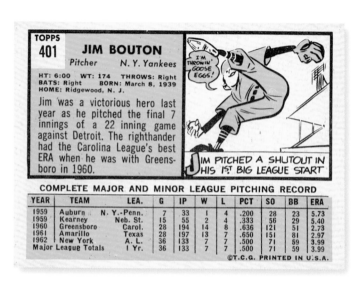

JIM BOUTON On the mound, the colorful Bouton enjoyed a couple of phenomenal seasons with the Yankees. At the typewriter, he authored *Ball Four*, the controversial 1970 bestseller that told behind-the-scenes clubhouse tales, rankling more than a few players. Following his 7–7 debut in 1962, Bouton turned in a sparkling 21–7 record in '63, with a career-high 148 strikeouts over 249.1 innings pitched, and made the All-Star squad. The right-hander came back the next season with an 18–13 mark, including a league-best 37 complete games. Arm injuries plagued Bouton the rest of his pitching career, though not his writing skills.

Topps card pictured: 1963 #401. The 1963 set includes the rookie card for Pete Rose, who is pictured with three other newcomers, including Yankees second baseman Pedro Gonzalez, who played 14 games for the Bombers that season.

JIM
BOUTON
NEW YORK YANKEES   P

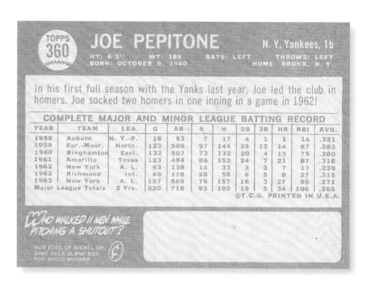

TOPPS 360

JOE PEPITONE

N. Y. Yankees, 1b

HT: 6'2"　　WT: 185　　BATS: LEFT　　THROWS: LEFT
BORN: OCTOBER 9, 1940　　　　HOME: BRONX, N. Y.

In his first full season with the Yanks last year, Joe led the club in homers. Joe socked two homers in one inning in a game in 1962!

COMPLETE MAJOR AND MINOR LEAGUE BATTING RECORD

YEAR	TEAM	LEA.	G	AB	R	H	2B	3B	HR	RBI	AVG.
1958	Auburn	N. Y.-P.	16	53	7	17	4	1	1	14	.321
1959	Far.-Moor.	North.	123	508	97	144	35	12	14	87	.283
1960	Binghamton	East.	132	507	73	132	20	4	13	75	.260
1961	Amarillo	Texas	123	484	86	153	24	7	21	87	.316
1962	New York	A. L.	63	138	14	33	3	2	7	17	.239
1962	Richmond	Int.	46	178	28	56	6	5	8	27	.315
1963	New York	A. L.	157	580	79	157	16	3	27	89	.271
	Major League Totals	2 Yrs.	220	718	93	190	19	5	34	106	.265

©T.C.G. PRINTED IN U.S.A.

WHO WALKED 11 MEN WHILE PITCHING A SHUTOUT?

RUB EDGE OF NICKEL OR
DIME OVER BLANK BOX
FOR MAGIC ANSWER

JOE PEPITONE　Pepitone—or Pepi, as the popular, fun-loving, Brooklyn-born power hitter became known among Yankees fans—showed enough potential during his part-time role in 1962 to earn the first baseman's job in '63 after the team traded Moose Skowron. Pepi rewarded that faith with an All-Star performance, batting .271 with 27 home runs and 89 RBIs. He followed up over the next three seasons with two more All-Star nods and a pair of Gold Gloves, along with 77 homers and 245 RBIs. Pepi played in the 1963 and '64 World Series, both Yankees losses, and remained an affable stalwart over the rest of the team's lackluster decade.

Topps card pictured: 1964 #360. The 1964 Topps Giants set had 60 oversize cards, each measuring 3⅛ inches by 5¼ inches, whose backs featured newspaper-style designs and stories.

YANKEES

JOE PEPITONE   **1st base**

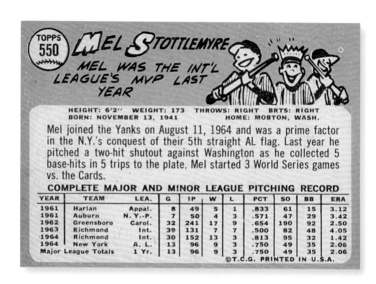

MEL STOTTLEMYRE

MEL WAS THE INT'L
LEAGUE'S MVP LAST
YEAR

HEIGHT: 6'2" WEIGHT: 173 THROWS: RIGHT BRTS: RIGHT
BORN: NOVEMBER 13, 1941 HOME: MOBTON, WASH.

Mel joined the Yanks on August 11, 1964 and was a prime factor in the N.Y.'s conquest of their 5th straight AL flag. Last year he pitched a two-hit shutout against Washington as he collected 5 base-hits in 5 trips to the plate. Mel started 3 World Series games vs. the Cards.

COMPLETE MAJOR AND MINOR LEAGUE PITCHING RECORD

YEAR	TEAM	LEA.	G	IP	W	L	PCT	SO	BB	ERA
1961	Harlan	Appal.	8	49	5	1	.833	61	15	3.12
1961	Auburn	N. Y.-P.	7	50	4	3	.571	47	29	3.42
1962	Greensboro	Carol.	32	241	17	9	.654	190	92	2.50
1963	Richmond	Int.	39	131	7	7	.500	82	48	4.05
1964	Richmond	Int.	30	152	13	3	.813	95	32	1.42
1964	New York	A. L.	13	96	9	3	.750	49	35	2.06
Major League Totals		1 Yr.	13	96	9	3	.750	49	35	2.06

©T.C.G. PRINTED IN U.S.A.

MEL STOTTLEMYRE If Stottlemyre had joined the Yankees at the beginning of their incredible run of five straight AL pennants, instead of at the end of that dynasty and the start of a long decline, he might have achieved even more greatness. Called up from the minors in August 1964, in the midst of a pennant chase, the unfazed rookie went 9–3 and pitched admirably in the World Series loss to St. Louis. He followed up with a 20–9 All-Star season, and but for a hiccup in '66, Stottlemyre was a winning workhorse before a torn rotator cuff ended his distinguished career.

Topps card pictured: 1965 #550. In 1965, collectors found gold-foil cards inserted in Topps wax packs. The 2⅛-inch-by-3½-inch inserts featured embossed profiles of 72 players, with red backgrounds for National Leaguers, blue for American Leaguers.

PITCHER

MEL STOTTLEMYRE

Wrapper for the 1970 Topps Super oversized (3⅛ by 5¼ inches) cards

PART 3 · 1970s

Compared with the 1960s, the '70s were a flip-flop for the Yankees, with a mediocre first half of the decade giving way to a resurgence in the second half. A harbinger of better days to come was Thurman Munson's Rookie of the Year campaign in 1970, while Bobby Murcer and Roy White, also homegrown talent, put up solid offensive numbers, too. Even so, after a second-place finish in the AL East in '70, the team muddled through the next four seasons.

During those years, however, trades netted some key players—reliever Sparky Lyle, third baseman Graig Nettles, first baseman Chris Chambliss, starters Dick Tidrow and Catfish Hunter, outfielder Lou Piniella—who would enjoy starring roles in the Yanks' revival. In another monumental development, the Yankees were purchased from CBS, which had owned the team since 1964, by a group headed by Cleveland shipping magnate George M. Steinbrenner in January 1973.

The team vacated Yankee Stadium for the 1974 and '75 seasons while the historic ballpark was being renovated, playing home games at Shea Stadium, the Mets home field, in Queens. And on August 1, 1975, former Yankee Billy Martin replaced manager Bill Virdon for what would be Martin's first of five stints as skipper.

All those elements combined to produce positive results in 1976, when the Yankees—glad to be back in their Bronx home at 168th Street and Broadway—snapped their long schneid and returned to the postseason. It happened in dramatic, storybook fashion when Chambliss, in the clinching game of the AL Championship Series against the Royals at the stadium, belted a walk-off home run. Although New York was swept by Cincinnati's Big Red Machine in the World Series, the Yanks got their winning mojo working again.

The free-agent signing of Reggie Jackson in 1976 proved pivotal to the Bronx Bombers' back-to-back world championships in 1977 and '78, highlighted by Mr. October's unprecedented trio of round-trippers in the Series winner against the Dodgers in 1977. A year later, Red Sox Nation began forever cursing Bucky "Bleeping" Dent's unexpected homer at Fenway Park that sent the Yanks back to the World Series and another victory over the Dodgers.

Topps baseball cards during the 1970s reflected the growth of the sport, the company, and the collecting hobby. There was the addition of American and National League Championship cards in 1970, player photos on card backs in '71, and "Traded" cards beginning in '72. In 1974, Topps issued all 660 cards at one time, instead of in consecutive series. In '75, to commemorate its 25th anniversary in baseball cards, the company issued 24 special cards picturing MVPs from 1951 to '74. The 1978 set included a whopping 726 cards.

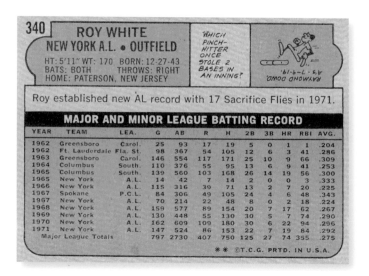

340 | **ROY WHITE**
NEW YORK A.L. • OUTFIELD

HT: 5'11" WT: 170 BORN: 12-27-43
BATS: BOTH THROWS: RIGHT
HOME: PATERSON, NEW JERSEY

WHICH
PINCH-
HITTER
ONCE
STOLE 2
BASES IN
AN INNING?

Roy established new AL record with 17 Sacrifice Flies in 1971.

MAJOR AND MINOR LEAGUE BATTING RECORD

YEAR	TEAM	LEA.	G	AB	R	H	2B	3B	HR	RBI	AVG.
1962	Greensboro	Carol.	25	93	17	19	5	0	1	1	.204
1962	Ft. Lauderdale	Fla. St.	98	367	54	105	12	6	3	41	.286
1963	Greensboro	Carol.	146	554	117	171	25	10	9	66	.309
1964	Columbus	South.	110	376	55	95	13	6	9	41	.253
1965	Columbus	South.	139	560	103	168	26	14	19	56	.300
1965	New York	A.L.	14	42	7	14	2	0	0	3	.333
1966	New York	A.L.	115	316	39	71	13	2	7	20	.225
1967	Spokane	P.C.L.	84	306	49	105	24	4	6	48	.343
1967	New York	A.L.	70	214	22	48	8	0	2	18	.224
1968	New York	A.L.	159	577	89	154	20	7	17	62	.267
1969	New York	A.L.	130	448	55	130	30	5	7	74	.290
1970	New York	A.L.	162	609	109	180	30	6	22	94	.296
1971	New York	A.L.	147	524	86	153	22	7	19	84	.292
	Major League Totals		797	2730	407	750	125	27	74	355	.275

✶ ✶ ©T.C.G. PRTD. IN U.S.A.

ROY WHITE White is revered by fans as the popular five-tool performer who buoyed the Yankees through their decade-long doldrums beginning in 1965 and helped them return to baseball's mountaintop with back-to-back World Series victories in 1977 and '78. The switch-hitter didn't stick full-time until 1968, when his all-around skills produced a .267 batting average, 17 home runs, 20 stolen bases, 89 runs, 73 base on balls, and near-flawless defense. White continued to put up spectacular offensive and defensive numbers—including the Yanks' first errorless season, in 1971—before highlighting his postseason play in 1978 with an AL Championship Series–clinching homer and a .333 batting average in the World Series.

Topps card pictured: 1972 #340. White, a switch-hitter, was noted for his distinct batting stance, which included pointing both feet inward. Hitting from the left side, as shown on this card, he kept his hands waist-high.

YANKEES

ROY WHITE

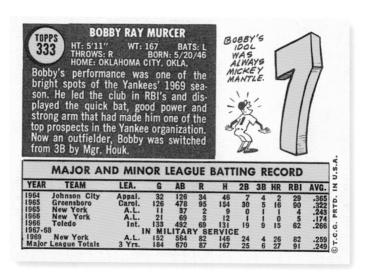

BOBBY MURCER Like his boyhood idol Mickey Mantle, Murcer was also a standout high school ballplayer in Oklahoma. So when Murcer joined the Yankees toward the end of Mantle's stellar career, it made sense that he was seen as the team's newest rising star. He was hoping to catch on as the starting shortstop in 1967, until the Army drafted him for its team for the next two years. Murcer returned in 1969, after the Mick's retirement, and the muscle he'd added in the military put more pop in his bat, leading to five straight seasons of 20-plus homers.

Topps card pictured: 1970 #333. The cartoon showing Murcer admiring the number 7 on the back of the card alludes to the fact that many considered him "the next Mickey Mantle," as both hailed from Oklahoma.

YANKS

Bobby Murcer | **OUTFIELD**

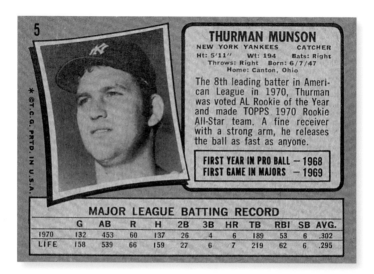

5

THURMAN MUNSON
NEW YORK YANKEES   **CATCHER**
Ht: 5'11"   Wt: 194   Bats: Right
Throws: Right   Born: 6/7/47
Home: Canton, Ohio

The 8th leading batter in American League in 1970, Thurman was voted AL Rookie of the Year and made TOPPS 1970 Rookie All-Star team. A fine receiver with a strong arm, he releases the ball as fast as anyone.

FIRST YEAR IN PRO BALL — 1968
FIRST GAME IN MAJORS — 1969

MAJOR LEAGUE BATTING RECORD

	G	AB	R	H	2B	3B	HR	TB	RBI	SB	AVG.
1970	132	453	60	137	26	4	6	189	53	6	.302
LIFE	158	539	66	159	27	6	7	219	62	6	.295

THURMAN MUNSON   While the tragic death of Munson in a plane crash in 1979 is still mourned among Yankees fans, he's more celebrated as one of the team's most beloved players. From his first full season in 1970, when he took Rookie of the Year honors, he became a stalwart on defense and offense. Munson was named team captain in 1976—the Yanks' first since Lou Gehrig—the same year New York returned to the World Series for the first time since 1964. Although they were swept by Cincinnati's Big Red Machine, Munson hit .529, then paced the Yankees to back-to-back Series titles in 1977 and '78.

Topps card pictured: 1971 #5. The Topps 1971 set marks the first time that players' photos, rather than cartoon likenesses, appeared on the back of the cards.

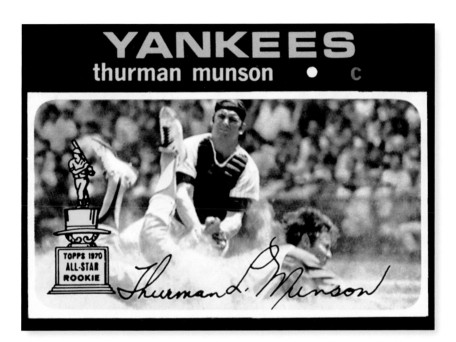

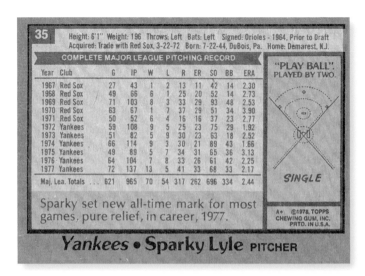

Year	Club	G	IP	W	L	R	ER	SO	BB	ERA
1967	Red Sox	27	43	1	2	13	11	42	14	2.30
1968	Red Sox	49	66	6	1	25	20	52	14	2.73
1969	Red Sox	71	103	8	3	33	29	93	48	2.53
1970	Red Sox	63	67	1	7	37	29	51	34	3.90
1971	Red Sox	50	52	6	4	16	16	37	23	2.77
1972	Yankees	59	108	9	5	25	23	75	29	1.92
1973	Yankees	51	82	5	9	30	23	63	18	2.52
1974	Yankees	66	114	9	3	30	21	89	43	1.66
1975	Yankees	49	89	5	7	34	31	65	36	3.13
1976	Yankees	64	104	7	8	33	26	61	42	2.25
1977	Yankees	72	137	13	5	41	33	68	33	2.17
Maj. Lea. Totals . . .		621	965	70	54	317	262	696	334	2.44

Height: 6'1" Weight: 196 Throws: Left Bats: Left Signed: Orioles - 1964, Prior to Draft Acquired: Trade with Red Sox, 3-22-72 Born: 7-22-44, DuBois, Pa. Home: Demarest, N.J.

COMPLETE MAJOR LEAGUE PITCHING RECORD

"PLAY BALL". PLAYED BY TWO.

SINGLE

Sparky set new all-time mark for most games, pure relief, in career, 1977.

A✶ ©1978, TOPPS CHEWING GUM, INC. PRTD. IN U.S.A.

Yankees • Sparky Lyle PITCHER

SPARKY LYLE Once he mastered his devastating slider to complement a decent fastball and curveball, Sparky overwhelmed hitters in his exclusive role as a reliever. He arrived in the Bronx via the Red Sox in 1972 and promptly established his indispensability by leading the league with 35 saves and a stingy 1.92 ERA. He topped the AL in saves again in '76—the year the Yanks' ended their interminable postseason drought—and pitched flawlessly in the World Series loss. He had a career year in 1977, finishing with 26 saves, a championship ring, and the AL Cy Young Award, the first ever for a reliever.

Topps card pictured: 1978 #35. The "Play Ball" game on the back of the 1978 cards challenged pairs of collectors to battle it out in a simulated baseball game.

P

Yankees

SPARKY LYLE

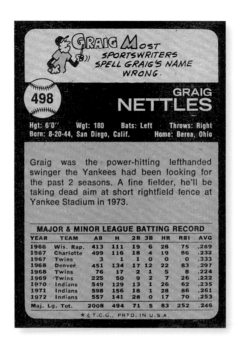

GRAIG Most
SPORTSWRITERS
SPELL GRAIG'S NAME
WRONG.

498

GRAIG
NETTLES

Hgt: 6'0"   Wgt: 180   Bats: Left   Throws: Right
Born: 8-20-44, San Diego, Calif.   Home: Berea, Ohio

Graig was the power-hitting lefthanded swinger the Yankees had been looking for the past 2 seasons. A fine fielder, he'll be taking dead aim at short rightfield fence at Yankee Stadium in 1973.

MAJOR & MINOR LEAGUE BATTING RECORD

YEAR	TEAM	AB	H	2B	3B	HR	RBI	AVG
1966	Wis. Rap.	413	111	19	6	28	75	.269
1967	Charlotte	499	116	18	4	19	86	.232
1967	Twins	3	1	1	0	0	0	.333
1968	Denver	451	134	17	12	22	83	.297
1968	Twins	76	17	2	1	5	8	.224
1969	Twins	225	50	9	2	7	26	.222
1970	Indians	549	129	13	1	26	62	.235
1971	Indians	598	156	18	1	28	86	.261
1972	Indians	557	141	28	0	17	70	.253
Maj. Lg. Tot.		2008	494	71	5	83	252	.246

★ C.T.C.G., PRTD. IN U.S.A.

GRAIG NETTLES After three seasons apiece with Minnesota and Cleveland, Nettles was traded to New York, where he established himself as a power-hitting, Gold Glove third baseman. He clubbed 250 home runs for the Yanks, including an AL-best 32 in 1976, when he helped boost the Bronx Bombers to the first of three straight World Series appearances. Nettles, who established the AL record for most homers by a third baseman (319), wasn't quite as productive in his postseason play with the Yanks, yet he made four unforgettable diving stops at the hot corner in Game 3 of the 1978 Series win over the Dodgers.

Topps card pictured: 1973 #498. Card #1 in the 1973 set pictured Babe Ruth, along with Hank Aaron and Willie Mays, as the "All Time Home Run Leaders."

GRAIG
NETTLES
NEW YORK YANKEES   3rd BASE

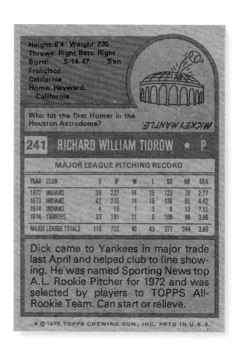

Height: 6'4" Weight: 220
Throws: Right Bats: Right
Born: 5-14-47. San
Francisco,
California
Home: Hayward,
California

Who hit the first Homer in the
Houston Astrodome? *MICKEY MANTLE*

241 RICHARD WILLIAM TIDROW ● P

MAJOR LEAGUE PITCHING RECORD

YEAR	CLUB	G	IP	W	L	SO	BB	ERA
1972	INDIANS	39	237	14	15	123	70	2.77
1973	INDIANS	42	275	14	16	138	95	4.42
1974	INDIANS	4	19	1	3	8	13	7.11
1974	YANKEES	33	191	11	9	108	66	3.86
MAJOR LEAGUE TOTALS		118	722	40	43	377	244	3.80

Dick came to Yankees in major trade
last April and helped club to fine showing. He was named Sporting News top
A.L. Rookie Pitcher for 1972 and was
selected by players to TOPPS All-
Rookie Team. Can start or relieve.

★ © 1975 TOPPS CHEWING GUM, INC. PRTD IN U.S.A.

DICK TIDROW Tidrow was a workhorse starter for the Indians, pitching 237.1 and 274.2 innings, respectively, in 1972 and '73. An early-season trade in '74 brought him, along with Chris Chambliss, to the Yankees. After an 11–9, 3.87 ERA season in the rotation, Tidrow moved to the bullpen for three seasons as the invaluable setup man for closer Sparky Lyle and a spot starter. Tidrow was actually the winner in the 1976 AL Championship Series clincher won on Chambliss's dramatic walk-off homer. In 1977, he went 11–4 with five saves—and 5–0 in seven starts—for the eventual World Series champs.

Topps card pictured: 1975 #241. Card #407 in the '75 set shows Oakland's Herb Washington in a base-running pose. It's the only Topps card to identify a player as "PR," or pinch-runner, and include just his base-running stats.

YANKEES

DICK TIDROW

Pitcher

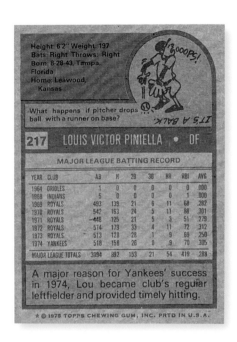

Height: 6'2" Weight: 197
Bats: Right Throws: Right
Born: 8-28-43, Tampa,
Florida
Home: Leawood,
Kansas

What happens if pitcher drops
ball with a runner on base?

IT'S A BALK.

217 LOUIS VICTOR PINIELLA • OF

MAJOR LEAGUE BATTING RECORD

YEAR	CLUB	AB	H	2B	3B	HR	RBI	AVG
1964	ORIOLES	1	0	0	0	0	0	.000
1968	INDIANS	5	0	0	0	0	1	.000
1969	ROYALS	493	139	21	6	11	68	.282
1970	ROYALS	542	163	24	5	11	88	.301
1971	ROYALS	448	125	21	5	3	51	.279
1972	ROYALS	574	179	33	4	11	72	.312
1973	ROYALS	513	128	28	1	9	69	.250
1974	YANKEES	518	158	26	0	9	70	.305
MAJOR LEAGUE TOTALS		3094	892	153	21	54	419	.288

A major reason for Yankees' success
in 1974, Lou became club's regular
leftfielder and provided timely hitting.

LOU PINIELLA A circuitous, five-team route finally landed Piniella in the Bronx in 1974, near the end of the team's decade-long slump. Sweet Lou immediately produced positive results, hitting .305 with 26 doubles and 70 RBIs. He would continue to hit for average (.295 over 11 seasons in New York) and hustle on the base paths and in left field. Teammate Bucky Dent is remembered for his decisive home run in the one-game playoff against the Red Sox in 1978 that won the Yanks the pennant, but two outstanding defensive plays by Piniella also proved pivotal. In four World Series with the Yanks, he hit .319.

Topps card pictured: 1975 #217. In 1975, Topps test-marketed a separate set of 660 mini cards, measuring 2¼ inches by 3⅛ inches, that were otherwise identical to those in the regular set. The mini set was distributed only on the West Coast and in Michigan.

YANKEES

LOU PINIELLA

Outfield

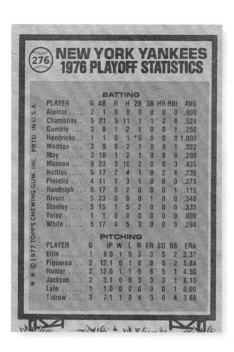

NEW YORK YANKEES
1976 PLAYOFF STATISTICS

(276)

©1977 TOPPS CHEWING GUM, INC. PRTD. IN U.S.A.

BATTING

PLAYER	G	AB	R	H	2B	3B	HR	RBI	AVG
Alomar	2	1	0	0	0	0	0	0	.000
Chambliss	5	21	5	11	1	1	2	8	.524
Gamble	3	8	1	2	1	0	0	1	.250
Hendricks	1	1	0	1	0	0	0	0	1.000
Maddox	3	9	0	2	1	0	0	1	.222
May	3	10	1	2	1	0	0	0	.200
Munson	5	23	3	10	2	0	0	3	.435
Nettles	5	17	2	4	1	0	2	4	.235
Piniella	4	11	1	3	1	0	0	0	.273
Randolph	5	17	0	2	0	0	0	1	.118
Rivers	5	23	5	8	0	1	0	0	.348
Stanley	5	15	1	5	2	0	0	0	.333
Velez	1	1	0	0	0	0	0	0	.000
White	5	17	4	5	3	0	0	3	.294

PITCHING

PLAYER	G	IP	W	L	R	ER	SO	BB	ERA
Ellis	1	8.0	1	0	3	3	5	2	3.37
Figueroa	2	12.1	0	1	8	8	5	2	5.84
Hunter	2	12.0	1	1	6	6	5	1	4.50
Jackson	2	3.1	0	0	3	3	3	1	8.10
Lyle	1	1.0	0	0	0	0	0	1	0.00
Tidrow	3	7.1	1	0	4	3	0	4	3.68

CHRIS CHAMBLISS   Yankee Stadium rocked as never before the night of October 14, 1976. That's when Chambliss, batting in the bottom of the ninth inning against the Kansas City Royals in the decisive Game 5 of the AL Championship Series with score tied 6–6, launched a ball over the outfield wall for one of the most dramatic walk-off home runs in postseason history. Chambliss had been traded to the Yankees from the Indians early in the 1974 season and eventually became a consistent run producer and home run threat, as well as a rock at first, winning a Gold Glove in 1978.

Topps card pictured: 1977 #276. The back of Chambliss's regular card in the '77 set (#220) refers to another big homer he hit in 1976: a two-out, bottom-of-the-ninth blast to cap a come-from-behind victory over the Red Sox on July 25.

A.L. CHAMPIONSHIP

1976

CHAMBLISS' DRAMATIC HOMER DECIDES IT

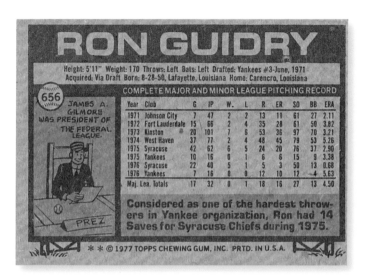

RON GUIDRY

Height: 5'11" Weight: 170 Throws: Left Bats: Left Drafted: Yankees #3-June, 1971
Acquired: Via Draft Born: 8-28-50, Lafayette, Louisiana Home: Carencro, Louisiana

656

JAMES A. GILMORE WAS PRESIDENT OF THE FEDERAL LEAGUE.

PREZ

COMPLETE MAJOR AND MINOR LEAGUE PITCHING RECORD

Year	Club	G	IP	W.	L	R	ER	SO	BB	ERA
1971	Johnson City	7	47	2	2	13	11	61	27	2.11
1972	Fort Lauderdale	15	66	2	4	35	28	61	50	3.82
1973	Kinston	20	101	7	6	53	36	97	70	3.21
1974	West Haven	37	77	2	4	48	45	79	53	5.26
1975	Syracuse	42	62	6	5	24	20	76	37	2.90
1975	Yankees	10	16	0	1	6	6	15	9	3.38
1976	Syracuse	22	40	5	1	5	3	50	13	0.68
1976	Yankees	7	16	0	0	12	10	12	4	5.63
Maj. Lea. Totals		17	32	0	1	18	16	27	13	4.50

Considered as one of the hardest throwers in Yankee organization, Ron had 14 Saves for Syracuse Chiefs during 1975.

✳ ✳ © 1977 TOPPS CHEWING GUM, INC. PRTD. IN U.S.A.

RON GUIDRY Guidry started the 1977 season as a reliever, but quickly moved into the starting rotation and turned in a solid season, with 16 wins against 7 losses and an impressive 2.82 ERA. That was just an appetizer, however, to his '78 campaign, one of the greatest ever by any pitcher. On his way to unanimously winning the Cy Young Award, Gator struck out 18 California Angels on June 17—still a Yankees record—and notched his ML-best 25th win in the historic one-game playoff against the archrival Red Sox. His filthy final figures: 25 wins, 3 losses, 9 shutouts, 248 strikeouts, and a 1.74 ERA.

Topps card pictured: 1977 #656. The key rookie cards from the '77 set are Dale Murphy (#476) and eventual Hall of Famer Andre Dawson (#473).

YANKEES
RON GUIDRY

JIM HUNTER PITCHER NEW YORK A.L.

100

HEIGHT: 6'0" WEIGHT: 195 THROWS: RIGHT BATS: RIGHT
SIGNED: A's-1964, PRIOR TO DRAFT ACQUIRED: FREE AGENT, 12-31-74
BORN: 4-8-46, HERTFORD, N.C. HOME: HERTFORD, N.C.

COMPLETE MAJOR LEAGUE PITCHING RECORD

YEAR	CLUB	G	IP	W	L	R	ER	SO	BB	ERA
1965	A's	32	133	8	8	68	63	82	46	4.26
1966	A's	30	177	9	11	87	79	103	64	4.02
1967	A's	35	260	13	17	91	81	196	84	2.80
1968	A's	36	234	13	13	99	87	172	69	3.35
1969	A's	38	247	12	15	99	92	150	85	3.35
1970	A's	40	262	18	14	124	111	178	74	3.81
1971	A's	37	274	21	11	103	90	181	80	2.96
1972	A's	38	295	21	7	74	67	191	70	2.04
1973	A's	36	256	21	5	105	95	124	69	3.34
1974	A's	41	318	25	12	97	88	143	46	2.49
1975	YANKEES	39	328	23	14	107	94	177	83	2.58
MAJ. LEA. TOTALS:		402	2784	184	127	1054	947	1697	770	3.06

● **Jim has been AL All-Star 7 times.**

© 1976 TOPPS CHEWING GUM, INC. PRTD. IN U.S.A.

CATFISH HUNTER By the time he came to the Yankees in 1975—after a contract dispute with A's owner Charlie Finley resulted in him becoming the first free agent of the modern era—Catfish was already a big-time winner. The author of a perfect game in 1968, the winner of the 1974 AL Cy Young Award, and a six-time All-Star, he'd led Oakland to three World Championships. Hunter won an AL-best 23 games his first year in pinstripes—the last of five straight seasons of 20-plus wins—then helped the Bombers win three AL championships in a row and the 1977 and '78 World Series.

Topps card pictured: 1976 #100. Catfish was featured on two other cards in the '76 set: "A.L. Victory Leaders 1975" (#200), with Jim Palmer and Vida Blue; and "Earned Run Avg Ldrs A.L. 1975" (#202), with Palmer and Dennis Eckersley.

JIM HUNTER

PITCHER **YANKEES**

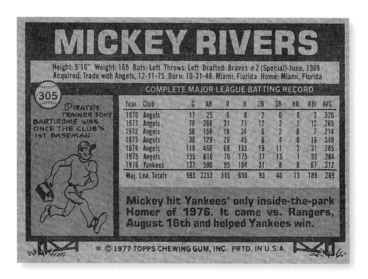

MICKEY RIVERS

Height: 5'10" Weight: 165 Bats: Left Throws: Left Drafted: Braves #2 (Special)-June, 1969
Acquired: Trade with Angels, 12-11-75 Born: 10-31-48, Miami, Florida Home: Miami, Florida

305

PIRATES' TRAINER TONY BARTIROME WAS ONCE THE CLUB'S 1ST BASEMAN.

COMPLETE MAJOR LEAGUE BATTING RECORD

Year	Club	G	AB	R	H	2B	3B	HR	RBI	AVG.
1970	Angels	17	25	6	8	2	0	0	3	.320
1971	Angels	78	268	31	71	12	2	1	12	.265
1972	Angels	58	159	18	34	6	2	0	7	.214
1973	Angels	30	129	26	45	6	4	0	16	.349
1974	Angels	118	466	69	133	19	11	3	31	.285
1975	Angels	155	616	70	175	17	13	1	53	.284
1976	Yankees	137	590	95	184	31	8	8	67	.312
Maj. Lea. Totals		593	2253	315	650	93	40	13	189	.289

Mickey hit Yankees' only inside-the-park Homer of 1976. It came vs. Rangers, August 16th and helped Yankees win.

✳ © 1977 TOPPS CHEWING GUM, INC. PRTD. IN U.S.A.

MICKEY RIVERS Although he only played three-plus seasons with the Yankees, Rivers was a sparkplug who helped ignite the team's three straight AL pennants and back-to-back World Series titles in 1977 and '78. Over his first two seasons in New York, leading off and hitting .312 and .326, respectively, he lived up to his nickname, Mick the Quick, not only by swiping 65 bases and legging out 20 triples but also by chasing down seemingly uncatchable balls in Yankee Stadium's expansive center field. Rivers enjoyed his finest postseason performance in 1978, hitting .455 in the AL Championship Series versus the Royals and .333 in the World Series win over the Dodgers.

Topps card pictured: 1977 #305. The 1977 set included four "Big League Brothers" cards (#631–#634), including one for siblings Paul and Rick Reuschel, both pitchers for the Cubs, that flip-flopped their IDs.

YANKEES

MICKEY RIVERS

OUTFIELD

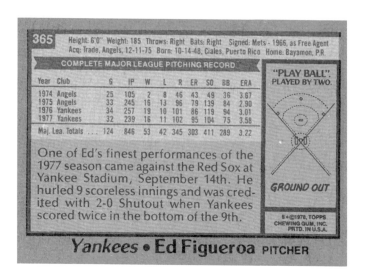

Year	Club	G	IP	W	L	R	ER	SO	BB	ERA
1974	Angels	25	105	2	8	46	43	49	36	3.67
1975	Angels	33	245	16	13	96	79	139	84	2.90
1976	Yankees	34	257	19	10	101	86	119	94	3.01
1977	Yankees	32	239	16	11	102	95	104	75	3.58
Maj. Lea. Totals ...		124	846	53	42	345	303	411	289	3.22

Height: 6'0" Weight: 185 Throws: Right Bats: Right Signed: Mets - 1966, as Free Agent
Acq: Trade, Angels, 12-11-75 Born: 10-14-48, Ciales, Puerto Rico Home: Bayamon, P.R.

COMPLETE MAJOR LEAGUE PITCHING RECORD

365

"PLAY BALL".
PLAYED BY TWO.

One of Ed's finest performances of the 1977 season came against the Red Sox at Yankee Stadium, September 14th. He hurled 9 scoreless innings and was credited with 2-0 Shutout when Yankees scored twice in the bottom of the 9th.

GROUND OUT

B • ©1978, TOPPS
CHEWING GUM, INC.
PRTD. IN U.S.A.

Yankees • Ed Figueroa PITCHER

ED FIGUEROA Figueroa's tenure in New York was brief though spectacular, for both the Yankees and the first Puerto Rican pitcher to win 20 games in a season (1978). He arrived in a December 1975 trade with the Angels that included Mickey Rivers, another key contributor to the Yanks. Figueroa anchored a resurgent Yankees pitching staff that brought back-to-back World Series titles to the Bronx in 1977 and '78 after a 12-year drought. From 1976 to '78, the right-hander won 55 games, including 38 complete games and eight shutouts, while posting a 3.18 ERA. Unfortunately, elbow surgery in 1979 virtually ended his career.

Topps card pictured: 1978 #365. Card #2 in the '78 set featured fellow Yankees pitcher Sparky Lyle as a "Record Breaker," lauding his 1977 season, for which he won the Cy Young Award.

Yankees

ED FIGUEROA

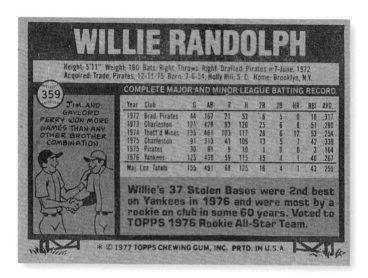

WILLIE RANDOLPH

Height: 5'11" Weight: 160 Bats: Right Throws: Right Drafted: Pirates #7-June, 1972
Acquired: Trade, Pirates, 12-11-75 Born: 7-6-54, Holly Hill, S. C. Home: Brooklyn, N.Y.

359

JIM AND GAYLORD PERRY WON MORE GAMES THAN ANY OTHER BROTHER COMBINATION.

COMPLETE MAJOR AND MINOR LEAGUE BATTING RECORD

Year	Club	G	AB	R	H	2B	3B	HR	RBI	AVG.
1972	Brad. Pirates	44	167	21	53	6	5	0	10	.317
1973	Charleston	121	428	93	120	25	6	8	51	.280
1974	Thett'd Mines	135	461	103	117	28	6	12	53	.254
1975	Charleston	91	313	41	106	13	5	7	42	.339
1975	Pirates	30	61	9	10	1	0	0	3	.164
1976	Yankees	125	430	59	115	15	4	1	40	.267
Maj. Lea. Totals		155	491	68	125	16	4	1	43	.255

Willie's 37 Stolen Bases were 2nd best on Yankees in 1976 and were most by a rookie on club in some 60 years. Voted to TOPPS 1976 Rookie All-Star Team.

✳ © 1977 TOPPS CHEWING GUM, INC. PRTD. IN U.S.A.

WILLIE RANDOLPH Randolph was a dynamic, stabilizing force on the field, as well as in a Bronx Zoo clubhouse full of talented if often raucous characters. An All-Star his first two seasons in pinstripes, Randolph displayed tremendous range at second base and an accurate arm. He hit for average and was always a threat to steal. Combined with his leadership skills—Randolph served as the Yankees captain from 1986 to '88—he was a stalwart on four AL pennant-winning teams in New York, two of which won it all. Randolph was later a coach with the Yankees dynasty that won four titles from 1996 to 2000.

Topps card pictured: 1977 #359. In 1977, Topps teamed up with Burger King franchises in the New York area to distribute a 24-card set featuring Yankees players. The design was the same as the regular set, though some photos were different. The Topps All-Star Rookie cup is not on Randolph's BK card.

YANKEES

WILLIE RANDOLPH

TOPPS
ALL-STAR ROOKIE

REGGIE JACKSON

Height: 6'0" Weight: 200 Bats: Left Throws: Left Drafted: A's #1-June, 1966
Acquired: Signed, Free Agent, 11-29-76 Born: 5-18-46, Wyncote Pa. Home: Tempe, Ariz.

10

PHIL RIZZUTO OFTEN PLACED CHEWED BUBBLE GUM ON BUTTON OF HIS CAP.

COMPLETE MAJOR LEAGUE BATTING RECORD

Year	Club	G	AB	R	H	2B	3B	HR	RBI	AVG.
1967	A's	35	118	13	21	4	4	1	6	.178
1968	A's	154	553	82	138	13	6	29	74	.250
1969	A's	152	549	123	151	36	3	47	118	.275
1970	A's	149	426	57	101	21	2	23	66	.237
1971	A's	150	567	87	157	29	3	32	80	.277
1972	A's	135	499	72	132	25	2	25	75	.265
1973	A's	151	539	99	158	28	2	32	117	.293
1974	A's	148	506	90	146	25	1	29	93	.289
1975	A's	157	593	91	150	39	3	36	104	.253
1976	Orioles	134	498	84	138	27	2	27	91	.277
Maj. Lea. Totals		1365	4848	798	1292	247	28	281	824	.267

Reggie tied for 2nd in Homers in A.L. in 1976 and was 10th best in R.B.I.'s.

* * © 1977 TOPPS CHEWING GUM, INC. PRTD. IN U.S.A.

REGGIE JACKSON Jackson was already a feared slugger when he joined the Yankees in 1977, and his five seasons in the Bronx solidified his reputation. He smacked 144 home runs with New York and averaged more than 100 RBIs in his four non-strike seasons there. Jackson's most remarkable performance, though, was in the '77 World Series versus the Dodgers. In the title-clinching Game 6, he clobbered three consecutive homers, all on the first pitch. He finished the Series with a record 5 dingers, 8 RBIs, and a .350 batting average—plus his immortal nickname, Mr. October.

Topps card pictured: 1977 #10. Topps actually produced another card for Jackson in 1977 that pictured him with the Orioles, but after he signed with the Yankees, that card was never printed. When proofs of the card were discovered, it created a stir in the collectors' market.

YANKEES
REGGIE JACKSON

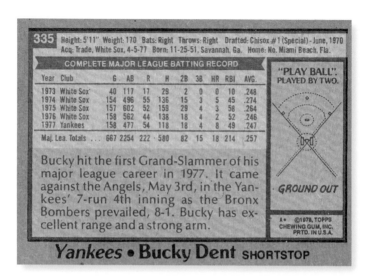

| 335 | Height: 5'11" Weight: 170 Bats: Right Throws: Right Drafted: Chisox #1 (Special) - June, 1970 | | | | | | | | |
| | Acq: Trade, White Sox, 4-5-77 Born: 11-25-51, Savannah, Ga. Home: No. Miami Beach, Fla. | | | | | | | | |

COMPLETE MAJOR LEAGUE BATTING RECORD

Year	Club	G	AB	R	H	2B	3B	HR	RBI	AVG.
1973	White Sox'	40	117	17	29	2	0	0	10	.248
1974	White Sox	154	496	55	136	15	3	5	45	.274
1975	White Sox	157	602	52	159	29	4	3	58	.264
1976	White Sox	158	562	44	138	18	4	2	52	.246
1977	Yankees	158	477	54	118	18	4	8	49	.247
Maj. Lea. Totals . . .		667	2254	222	· 580	82	15	18	214	.257

Bucky hit the first Grand-Slammer of his major league career in 1977. It came against the Angels, May 3rd, in the Yankees' 7-run 4th inning as the Bronx Bombers prevailed, 8-1. Bucky has excellent range and a strong arm.

"PLAY BALL".
PLAYED BY TWO.

GROUND OUT

A★ ©1978, TOPPS
CHEWING GUM, INC.
PRTD. IN U.S.A.

Yankees • **Bucky Dent** SHORTSTOP

BUCKY DENT Dent came to the Yankees from the White Sox in 1977 as a sure-handed shortstop—he was second in the 1974 Rookie of the Year balloting and an All-Star in '75—and, with Willie Randolph at second, provided superb up-the-middle defense during the Yanks' championship seasons in 1977 and '78. Considered a potent though light hitter, he flashed unexpected power by driving a ball just over Fenway Park's Green Monster in the one-game playoff that sent the Bombers to the 1978 postseason. Dent went on to hit .417 with seven RBIs in the World Series win over Los Angeles and was named the Series MVP.

Topps card pictured: 1978 #335. The 1978 set includes 11 rookie cards, with four freshmen on each, by position. Dale Murphy is featured as a catcher (#708), though over 14 seasons he played only 85 of 1,853 games behind the plate.

SS

Yankees

BUCKY DENT

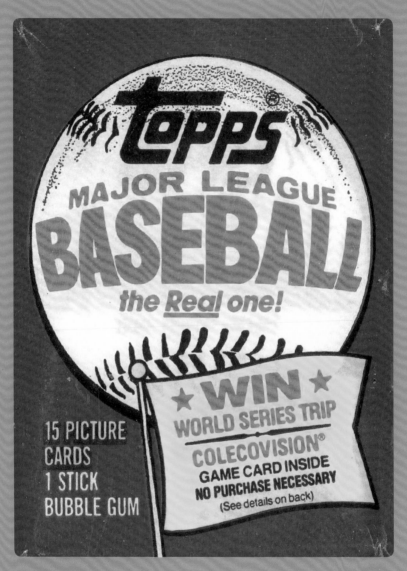

1982 wrapper

PART 4 · 1980s

The Yankees won 103 games in 1980 to capture the AL East flag and seemed poised to make another title run, but the Royals had other ideas. George Brett and company avenged three straight AL Championship Series losses to New York, from 1976 to '78, sweeping the Bombers in three games this time around. A 50-day, midsummer player strike discombobulated the '81 season, resulting in first- and second-half winners and an odd playoff system. The Dodgers and Yankees made it to the World Series, with Los Angeles overcoming a 0–2 start to win the championship in six games.

The rest of the decade produced memorable performances by great players—Dave Righetti's no-hitter versus Boston in 1983, Don Mattingly's MVP season in '85, Rickey Henderson's electricity every time he stepped into the batter's box, Dave Winfield's phenomenal offensive numbers year after year—yet no postseason appearances. The managerial merry-go-round kept the Yanks on the back covers of the city's tabloids, but didn't help matters much on the field. Still, the Yankees always kept their fans' "wait till next season" hopefulness alive.

Keeping fans' flames flickering were the Topps cards that pictured their favorite Yankees every year. The collecting hobby continued its meteoric rise during the 1980s, and Topps remained at the forefront with a slew of innovations. In 1981, for instance, the largest set to date included not only 726 "regular" cards but also 132 Traded ones. Super Action Cards, featuring action photos of 40 of the game's tops stars, highlighted the '82 set. In 1985, Topps reprised its popular Father & Son cards, which debuted in 1976, including Yogi Berra and his son Dale, who is pictured in a Pirates uniform even though he had been traded to the Yanks before the '85 season. In 1989, Topps revived the Bowman brand, with a heavy emphasis on rookies.

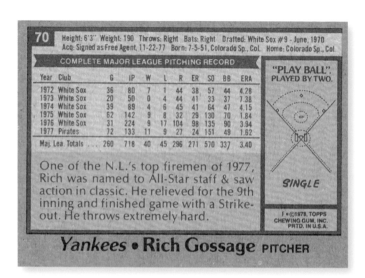

| 70 | Height: 6'3" Weight: 190 Throws: Right Bats: Right Drafted: White Sox #9 - June, 1970 |
| | Acq: Signed as Free Agent, 11-22-77 Born: 7-5-51, Colorado Sp., Col. Home: Colorado Sp., Col. |

COMPLETE MAJOR LEAGUE PITCHING RECORD

"PLAY BALL".
PLAYED BY TWO.

Year	Club	G	IP	W	L	R	ER	SO	BB	ERA
1972	White Sox	36	80	7	1	44	38	57	44	4.28
1973	White Sox	20	50	0	4	44	41	33	37	7.38
1974	White Sox	39	89	4	6	45	41	64	47	4.15
1975	White Sox	62	142	9	8	32	29	130	70	1.84
1976	White Sox	31	224	9	17	104	98	135	90	3.94
1977	Pirates	72	133	11	9	27	24	151	49	1.62
Maj. Lea. Totals . . .		260	718	40	45	296	271	570	337	3.40

One of the N.L.'s top firemen of 1977, Rich was named to All-Star staff & saw action in classic. He relieved for the 9th inning and finished game with a Strike-out. He throws extremely hard.

SINGLE

F ★ ©1978, TOPPS
CHEWING GUM, INC.
PRTD. IN U.S.A.

Yankees • **Rich Gossage** PITCHER

GOOSE GOSSAGE Over his 22 seasons as an intimidating, dominating, flame-throwing reliever, Gossage pitched for nine different teams, though the Yankees years from 1978 to '83 marked the zenith of his Hall of Fame career. Throughout those six campaigns—which began auspiciously with 27 regular-season saves and a World Series ring—Goose defined "workhorse." Appearing in 308 games, over which he hurled 518.2 innings, he led the AL in saves twice (27 in '78, 33 in '80) for a total of 150, nearly half his career tally. Doing the math tells you that unlike modern-day closers, Goose often worked two or even three innings in securing wins.

Topps card pictured: 1978 #70. The 1978 set is highly valued for its three Reggie Jackson cards, which document his amazing '77 season, including his three-homer World Series Game 6.

RICH GOSSAGE

| 690 | PITCHER **Tommy John** YANKEES |

TOMMY LED NATIONAL LEAGUE WITH .696 WON-LOST PERCENTAGE FOR THE DODGERS IN 1973.

COMPLETE MAJOR LEAGUE PITCHING RECORD

Year	Club	G	IP	W	L	R	ER	SO	BB	ERA
1963	Indians	6	20	0	2	10	5	9	6	2.25
1964	Indians	25	94	2	9	53	41	65	35	3.93
1965	White Sox	39	184	14	7	67	63	126	58	3.08
1966	White Sox	34	223	14	11	76	65	138	57	2.62
1967	White Sox	31	178	10	13	62	49	110	47	2.48
1968	White Sox	25	177	10	5	45	39	117	49	1.98
1969	White Sox	33	232	9	11	91	84	128	90	3.26
1970	White Sox	37	269	12	17	117	98	138	101	3.28
1971	White Sox	38	229	13	16	115	92	131	58	3.62
1972	Dodgers	29	187	11	5	68	60	117	40	2.89
1973	Dodgers	36	218	16	7	88	75	116	50	3.10
1974	Dodgers	22	153	13	3	51	44	78	42	2.59
1975	Dodgers				On Disabled List					
1976	Dodgers	31	207	10	10	76	71	91	61	3.09
1977	Dodgers	31	220	20	7	82	68	123	50	2.78
1978	Dodgers	33	213	17	10	95	78	124	53	3.30
1979	Yankees	37	276	21	9	109	91	111	65	2.97
Major Lea. Totals	....	487	3080	192	142	1205	1023	1722	862	2.99

D★ ©1980. TOPPS CHEWING GUM, INC. PRTD. IN U.S.A.

Height: 6'3'' **Weight:** 185 **Throws:** Left **Bats:** Right **Signed:** Indians-1961, Prior to Draft
Acquired: Signed, Free Agent, 11-21-78 **Born:** 5-22-43, Terre Haute, Ind. **Home:** Yorba Linda, Cal.

TOMMY JOHN The first of John's 288 career wins came when Pete Rose was a rookie; his last came during Ken Griffey Jr.'s first MLB year. The loquacious lefty arrived for his initial stint in the Bronx with a surgically repaired left elbow—from a 1975 tendon-swapping procedure, today known as "Tommy John surgery"—that gave new life to his sinking fastball. He finished his first two Yankees seasons at 21–7 and 22–7, respectively, over a total 541.2 innings that produced 23 complete games and nine shutouts. A 43-year-old John returned to the Yanks in 1986; a year later he led the staff with 187.2 innings pitched.

Topps card pictured: 1980 #690. In addition to the 726 cards in its regular set, the company issued a 60-card Topps Super set, wrapped in cellophane packs. The oversize cards measured 5 by 7 inches and featured a facsimile autograph over each player's photo—including John's (#23).

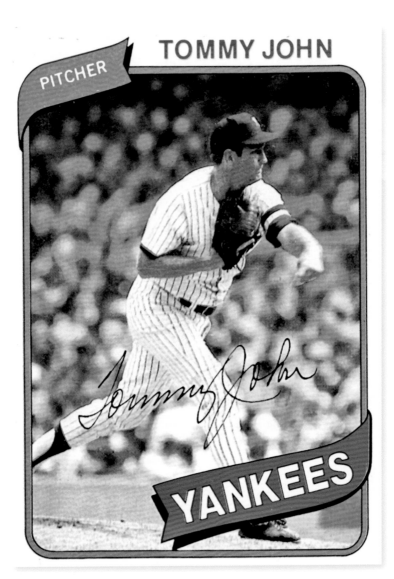

TOMMY JOHN

PITCHER

YANKEES

DAVE WINFIELD   Winfield's size (6-foot-6, 220 pounds) and superb ath-
leticism helped him excel in three sports at the University of Minnesota, resulting in him being drafted by the NBA, ABA, NHL, and MLB. He signed with the
San Diego Padres and went straight to the majors. He was already a superstar
when the Yankees signed him to an unprecedented 10-year deal, and although
his tenure in pinstripes proved tumultuous, as he and George Steinbrenner
feuded, his production was outstanding. From 1982 to '86, he averaged 108
RBIs, 30 doubles, and 28 home runs while hitting .288. His .340 batting average in 1984 was .003 shy of the AL's best, owned by teammate Don Mattingly.

Topps card pictured: 1985 #705. A highlight of the '85 set are 16 cards (#389–#404) featuring mem-
bers of the 1984 U.S. Olympic baseball team that won the gold medal, including Mark McGwire, Oddibe
McDowell, and Shane Mack.

DAVE WINFIELD
OUTFIELD
AL

ALL STAR

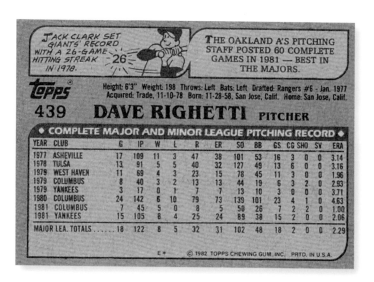

DAVE RIGHETTI Righetti came up as a promising left-handed starter, and he immediately showed his immense potential with a Rookie of the Year performance in 1981, finishing 8–4 in 15 starts with a 2.05 ERA. And although he twirled a no-hitter against the Red Sox on July 4, 1983, his Yankees destiny would be as one of the game's top closers during his tenure in the Bronx. After moving to the bullpen in 1984, Rags averaged 32 saves over the ensuing seven seasons—including a then-MLB-record 46 in 1986—with a 2.96 ERA, 506 shutouts, and a nearly 2-to-1 strikeouts-to-walks ratio.

Topps card pictured: 1982 #439. A subset of "In Action" cards, featuring 40 star players, was a big hit in 1982. Among those pictured was Yankees slugger Reggie Jackson (#301).

YANKEES
topps
DAVE RIGHETTI
PITCHER

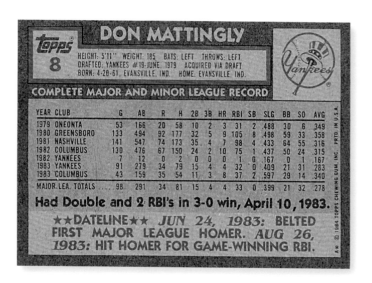

DON MATTINGLY

Topps
8

HEIGHT: 5'11" WEIGHT: 185 BATS: LEFT THROWS: LEFT
DRAFTED: YANKEES #19-JUNE, 1979 ACQUIRED VIA DRAFT
BORN: 4-20-61, EVANSVILLE, IND. HOME: EVANSVILLE, IND.

Yankees

COMPLETE MAJOR AND MINOR LEAGUE RECORD

YEAR CLUB	G	AB	R	H	2B	3B	HR	RBI	SB	SLG	BB	SO	AVG
1979 ONEONTA	53	166	20	58	10	2	3	31	2	.488	30	6	.349
1980 GREENSBORO	133	494	92	177	32	5	9	105	8	.498	59	33	.358
1981 NASHVILLE	141	547	74	173	35	4	7	98	4	.433	64	55	.316
1982 COLUMBUS	130	476	67	150	24	2	10	75	1	.437	50	24	.315
1982 YANKEES	7	12	0	2	0	0	0	1	0	.167	0	1	.167
1983 YANKEES	91	279	34	79	15	4	4	32	0	.409	21	31	.283
1983 COLUMBUS	43	159	35	54	11	3	8	37	2	.597	29	14	.340
MAJOR LEA. TOTALS	98	291	34	81	15	4	4	33	0	.399	21	32	.278

Had Double and 2 RBI's in 3-0 win, April 10, 1983.

★★DATELINE★★ *JUN 24, 1983:* BELTED FIRST MAJOR LEAGUE HOMER. *AUG 26, 1983:* HIT HOMER FOR GAME-WINNING RBI.

DON MATTINGLY During 14 years in pinstripes, the Hit Man earned his moniker by amassing incredible offensive numbers, highlighted by his 1985 MVP season, when he set major-league marks—that still stand—for the most consecutive games hitting at least one home run (eight) and the most grand slams in a season (six). He also paced the AL that year with 48 doubles and 145 RBIs. An outstanding defensive player, too, he won nine Gold Gloves and led AL first basemen in fielding percentage four times. Mattingly retired after the 1995 season as one of the team's most beloved stars ever. Proof: His number 23 was retired in '97.

Topps card pictured: 1984 #8. In 1984, as a send-away premium, Nestlé released 792 cards in uncut sheets that were almost identical to the Topps base set.

YANKEES

topps ®

DON
MATTINGLY OF-1B

1985 AL LEADERS

ON-BASE PERCENTAGE

Player	Team	Pct.
Wade Boggs	Red Sox	.450
George Brett	Royals	.436
Toby Harrah	Rangers	.432
RICKEY HENDERSON	**YANKEES**	**.419**
Eddie Murray	Orioles	.383
Willie Randolph	Yankees	.382
Alvin Davis	Mariners	.381
Dwight Evans	Red Sox	.378
Brett Butler	Indians	.377
Rod Carew	Angels	.371

Rickey Henderson
ALL-STAR OUTFIELDER

Hit 2 Homers at Detroit, 6-21-85. His leadoff Homer produced Game-Winning RBI, 10-3-85. Set Yankees mark with 80 Stolen Bases in 1985.

© 1986 TOPPS CHEWING GUM, INC. PRTD. IN U.S.A

RICKEY HENDERSON The four-plus seasons Henderson spent with the Yankees were a microcosm of his high-octane, prolific Hall of Fame career. Statistically the greatest leadoff hitter ever, he would get on base, steal a bag or two, and score. His lightning speed and aggressiveness helped him get to balls in left field that few others might reach, but more so to tear around the base paths. The Man of Steal broke or set a slew of stolen-base records, including the single-season mark (130 in 1982) and MLB career record. He also set career marks for most runs (2,295) and leadoff home runs (81).

Topps card pictured: 1986 #716. Rickey's selection to the 1985 AL All-Star team was the fifth of his 10 appearances in the Midsummer Classic.

RICKEY HENDERSON

A.L. ALL STAR

OF

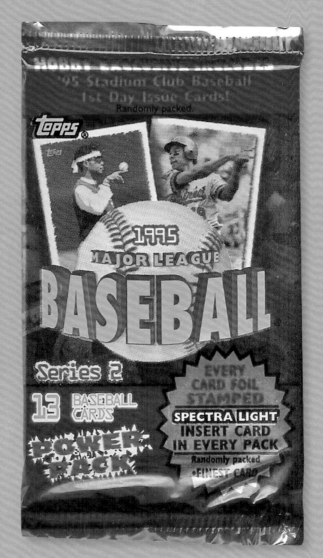

1995 foil pack

PART 5 · 1990s

The first three seasons of the 1990s were not kind to the Yankees. While Don Mattingly remained one of baseball's best players, he simply didn't have enough support, especially after Dave Winfield's tumultuous tenure in the Bronx ended with a trade to the Angels in May 1990. A paucity of pitching didn't help, either. Midway through the decade, though, things began to turn around.

The arrival of homegrown talent—Bernie Williams, Derek Jeter, Jorge Posada, Andy Pettitte, and Mariano Rivera—propelled the reversal of fortunes. Free agency and trades brought Paul O'Neill, Jimmy Key, Wade Boggs, David Cone, John Wetteland, and Darryl Strawberry to the Bronx. The Yanks owned the AL's best record in 1994 before the catastrophic players' strike, enacted on August 12, derailed not only that regular season and playoffs but also the early part of the next season. The team's talent kept growing in '95, and the Yanks became the AL's first wild-card postseason qualifier. Although they lost a thrilling five-game series to the Mariners, a new Yankees dynasty was emerging.

In 1996, New York won the AL East for the first time since 1980, then endured three nail-biting playoff series before bringing the World Series trophy back to the Bronx with a six-game victory over the Braves. Following another wild-card spot in the '97 postseason,

they were knocked off in the Divisional Series by the Indians. The 1998 Yankees won a regular-season-record 114 games—including David Wells's perfect game on May 17—then rambled through a postseason capped off with a sweep of the Padres in the World Series.

The Bronx Bombers continued their onslaught in '99, posting a 98–64 record—as well as another perfect game, tossed by David Cone on Yogi Berra Day, July 18—and yet another World Series sweep, this time against Atlanta. While closing out the 20th century in fantastic fashion, the Yankees also experienced sad moments that year. On March 8, Joe DiMaggio passed away, and on September 9, Catfish Hunter lost his valiant battle with cancer.

Yankees fans had a rash of rookie cards to amass throughout the 1990s, and Topps issues topped many collections. Although bubble gum and wax packs disappeared, many exciting features took up the slack. There were bronze mini-replicas, a card picturing President George H. W. Bush playing baseball at Yale, and Stadium Club and Topps Finest cards. The company celebrated its 40th anniversary in 1991, with special cards and giveaways. Topps Magazine, published quarterly from 1990 to '94, included a sheet of exclusive cards inside. In 1995, there was a Bazooka 132-card set and 59 3-D cards.

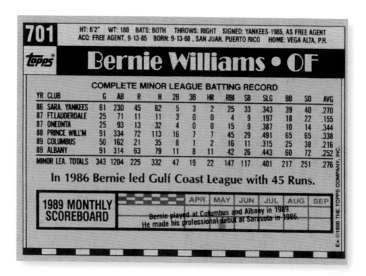

701

HT: 6'2" WT: 180 BATS: BOTH THROWS: RIGHT SIGNED: YANKEES-1985, AS FREE AGENT
ACQ: FREE AGENT, 9-13-85 BORN: 9-13-68 , SAN JUAN, PUERTO RICO HOME: VEGA ALTA, P.R.

Bernie Williams • OF

COMPLETE MINOR LEAGUE BATTING RECORD

YR	CLUB	G	AB	R	H	2B	3B	HR	RBI	SB	SLG	BB	SO	AVG
86	SARA. YANKEES	61	230	45	62	5	3	2	25	33	.343	39	40	.270
87	FT. LAUDERDALE	25	71	11	11	3	0	0	4	9	.197	18	22	.155
87	ONEONTA	25	93	13	32	4	0	0	15	9	.387	10	14	.344
88	PRINCE WILL'M	91	334	72	113	16	7	7	45	29	.491	65	65	.338
89	COLUMBUS	50	162	21	35	8	1	2	16	11	.315	25	38	.216
89	ALBANY	91	314	63	79	11	8	11	42	26	.443	60	72	.252
MINOR LEA. TOTALS		343	1204	225	332	47	19	22	147	117	.401	217	251	.276

In 1986 Bernie led Gulf Coast League with 45 Runs.

1989 MONTHLY SCOREBOARD

	APR	MAY	JUN	JUL	AUG	SEP

Bernie played at Columbus and Albany in 1989.
He made his professional debut at Sarasota in 1986.

E★ ©1990 THE TOPPS COMPANY, INC.

BERNIE WILLIAMS Williams followed in the grand Yankees tradition of prolific center fielders—including DiMaggio, Mantle, and Rivers—providing not just deft defense but also omnipresent offense. The switch-hitter batted over .300 eight straight seasons (1995–2002), a stretch during which he notched a batting title (for his .339 batting average in 1998), drove in 100 or more runs five times, and averaged 32 doubles and 24 home runs. Williams went to the postseason each of those years, appearing in 121 playoff games that culminated in five AL pennants and four World Series titles. In 1999, the third of his five straight All-Star campaigns, Bernie hit a career-high .342.

Topps card pictured: 1990 #701. Along with Bernie's rookie card, the 1990 set included those of fellow future superstars Frank Thomas (#414), Juan Gonzalez (#331), Sammy Sosa (#692), and Larry Walker (#757).

YANKEES

Topps

BERNIE WILLIAMS

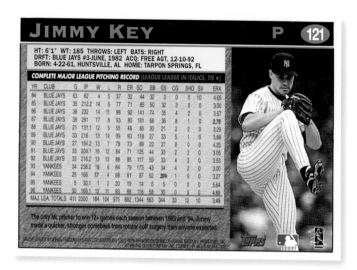

JIMMY KEY P 121

HT: 6'1" WT: 185 THROWS: LEFT BATS: RIGHT
DRFT: BLUE JAYS #3-JUNE, 1982 ACQ: FREE AGT, 12-10-92
BORN: 4-22-61, HUNTSVILLE, AL HOME: TARPON SPRINGS, FL

COMPLETE MAJOR LEAGUE PITCHING RECORD (LEAGUE LEADER IN ITALICS, TIE ♦)

YR	CLUB	G	IP	W	L	R	ER	SO	BB	GS	CG	SHO	SV	ERA
84	BLUE JAYS	63	62	4	5	37	32	44	32	0	0	0	10	4.65
85	BLUE JAYS	35	212.2	14	6	77	71	85	50	32	3	0	0	3.00
86	BLUE JAYS	36	232	14	11	98	92	141	74	35	4	2	0	3.57
87	BLUE JAYS	36	261	17	8	93	80	161	66	36	8	1	0	2.76
88	BLUE JAYS	21	131.1	12	5	55	48	65	30	21	2	2	0	3.29
89	BLUE JAYS	33	216	13	14	99	93	118	27	33	5	1	0	3.88
90	BLUE JAYS	27	154.2	13	7	79	73	88	22	27	0	0	0	4.25
91	BLUE JAYS	33	209.1	16	12	84	71	125	44	33	2	2	0	3.05
92	BLUE JAYS	33	216.2	13	13	88	85	117	59	33	4	2	0	3.53
93	YANKEES	34	236.2	18	6	84	79	173	43	34	4	2	0	3.00
94	YANKEES	25	168	17	4	68	61	97	52	25♦	1	0	0	3.27
95	YANKEES	5	30.1	1	2	20	19	14	6	5	0	0	0	5.64
96	YANKEES	30	169.1	12	11	93	88	116	58	30	0	0	0	4.68
MAJ. LEA. TOTALS		411	2300	164	104	975	892	1344	563	344	33	12	10	3.49

The only AL pitcher to win 12+ games each season between 1985 and '94, Jimmy
made a quicker, stronger comeback from rotator cuff surgery than anyone expected.

JIMMY KEY Key was a remarkably consistent winner throughout his career, only once finishing below .500 as a full-time starter. His tenure in the Bronx epitomized Key's value. Arriving as a free agent in '93, after back-to-back world championships with Toronto, he went 18–6. Key led the AL with a 17–4 record in the strike-shortened 1994 season, then missed most of '95 following rotator cuff surgery. Despite two stints on the disabled list in 1986, he gutted out a 12–11 record as the Yankees went to their first World Series since 1981 and was the winning pitcher in the clinching Game 6 versus Atlanta.

Topps card pictured: 1997 #121. The 1997 set featured a special subset of 27 Willie Mays reprint cards, including those issued by both Topps and Bowman. Cards autographed by Mays were randomly inserted in Series 1 packs.

JIMMY KEY

Paul O'Neill

HT: 6'4" WT: 215 BATS: LEFT THROWS: LEFT
DRFT: REDS #4-JUNE, 1981 ACQ: TRADE, 11-3-92
BORN: 2-25-63, COLUMBUS, OH HOME: CINCINNATI, OH

COMPLETE MAJOR LEAGUE BATTING RECORD
(LEAGUE LEADER IN *ITALICS*, TIE ✦)

YR	CLUB	G	AB	R	H	2B	3B	HR	RBI	SB	SLG	BB	SO	AVG
85	REDS	5	12	1	4	1	0	0	1	0	.417	0	2	.333
86	REDS	3	2	0	0	0	0	0	0	0	.000	1	1	.000
87	REDS	84	160	24	41	14	1	7	28	2	.488	18	29	.256
88	REDS	145	485	58	122	25	3	16	73	8	.414	38	65	.252
89	REDS	117	428	49	118	24	2	15	74	20	.446	46	64	.276
90	REDS	145	503	59	136	28	0	16	78	13	.421	53	103	.270
91	REDS	152	532	71	136	36	0	28	91	12	.481	73	107	.256
92	REDS	148	496	59	122	19	1	14	66	6	.373	77	85	.246
93	YANKEES	141	498	71	155	34	1	20	75	2	.504	44	69	.311
94	YANKEES	103	368	68	132	25	1	21	83	5	.603	72	56	.359
MAJ. LEA. TOTALS		1043	3484	460	966	206	9	137	569	68	.460	422	581	.277

After Opening Day, it was June 18 until Paul entered a game below .400 en route to his batting crown. He is a brother of Molly O'Neill, the acclaimed NY Times food writer.

MAJOR LEAGUE BASEBALL TRADEMARKS AND COPYRIGHTS ARE USED WITH PERMISSION OF MAJOR LEAGUE BASEBALL PROPERTIES, INC.
© 1995 THE TOPPS COMPANY, INC. LICENSED BY MLB & MLBPA, 1995
DIAMOND VISION ® IS A REGISTERED TRADEMARK OF MITSUBISHI ELECTRIC CORPORATION

426

PAUL O'NEILL George Steinbrenner nicknamed O'Neill "the "Warrior," and for good reason. Traded from the Reds after the 1991 season, O'Neill roamed right field for the next nine years, darting and diving for balls with reckless abandon and flawless results. In fact, he played 235 consecutive games (part of 1995, all of '96, and part of '97) without making an error. O'Neill was a battler at the plate and on the base paths, too, known for legging out doubles and working pitchers deep into counts. He continues to impress Yankees fans as a member of the YES Network broadcast crew.

Topps card pictured: 1995 #426. In the wake of the 1994 players' strike, Topps included a subset in '95 featuring "Cyberstats," described on card backs as "computer-simulated data for games of August 12, 1994 through the scheduled conclusion of the 1994 season."

Paul O'Neill

OF—NEW YORK YANKEES

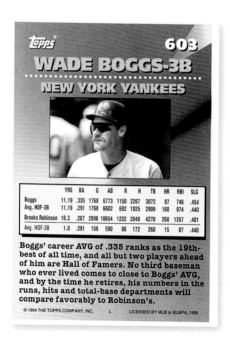

	YRS	BA	G	AB	R	H	TB	HR	RBI	SLG
Boggs	11.19	.335	1768	6773	1150	2267	3072	87	746	.454
Avg. HOF-3B	11.19	.291	1768	6602	692	1925	2909	168	974	.440
Brooks Robinson	18.3	.267	2896	10654	1232	2848	4270	268	1357	.401
Avg. HOF-3B	1.0	.291	158	590	86	172	260	15	87	.440

Boggs' career AVG of .335 ranks as the 19th-best of all time, and all but two players ahead of him are Hall of Famers. No third baseman who ever lived comes to close to Boggs' AVG, and by the time he retires, his numbers in the runs, hits and total-base departments will compare favorably to Robinson's.

© 1994 THE TOPPS COMPANY, INC.   L   LICENSED BY MLB & MLBPA, 1994

WADE BOGGS   Boggs, a perennial All-Star and five-time batting champ with the Red Sox, was already Cooperstown bound when he signed with the Yankees in 1993. He continued producing All-Star results, hitting .300-plus four straight seasons and earning two Gold Gloves. The elusive goal, though, was a World Series ring; yet that awaited once New York made the 1996 postseason. He platooned at third in victories over Texas and Baltimore and in the Fall Classic against Atlanta. Ironically, Boggs's bases-loaded walk won Game 4 and tied the Series. After the Yanks won in six games, a triumphant Boggs paraded around Yankee Stadium on an NYPD horse.

Topps card pictured: 1994 #603. Boggs was among nine players included in a subset previewing the 1994 set. The horizontal card #390 pictured Boggs attempting to turn a double play; the card back had a box stating, "Pre-production sample. Design and photo selection subject to change."

MEASURES OF GREATNESS

WADE BOGGS

Topps

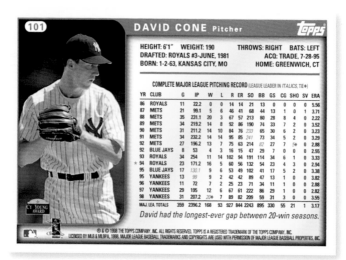

| | | | DAVID CONE Pitcher | | | | | | | | Topps | | | |

HEIGHT: 6'1" **WEIGHT: 190** **THROWS: RIGHT** **BATS: LEFT**
DRAFTED: ROYALS #3-JUNE, 1981 **ACQ: TRADE, 7-28-95**
BORN: 1-2-63, KANSAS CITY, MO **HOME: GREENWICH, CT**

COMPLETE MAJOR LEAGUE PITCHING RECORD (LEAGUE LEADER IN *ITALICS*, TIE◆)

YR	CLUB	G	IP	W	L	R	ER	SO	BB	GS	CG	SHO	SV	ERA
86	ROYALS	11	22.2	0	0	14	14	21	13	0	0	0	0	5.56
87	METS	21	99.1	5	6	46	41	68	44	13	1	0	1	3.71
88	METS	35	231.1	20	3	67	57	213	80	28	8	4	0	2.22
89	METS	34	219.2	14	8	92	86	190	74	33	7	2	0	3.52
90	METS	31	211.2	14	10	84	76	*233*	65	30	6	2	0	3.23
91	METS	34	232.2	14	14	95	85	*241*	73	34	5	2	0	3.29
92	METS	27	196.2	13	7	75	63	214	*82*	27	7	5◆	0	2.88
92	BLUE JAYS	8	53	4	3	16	15	47	29	7	0	0	0	2.55
93	ROYALS	34	254	11	14	102	94	191	114	34	6	1	0	3.33
★ 94	ROYALS	23	171.2	16	5	60	56	132	54	23	4	3	0	2.94
95	BLUE JAYS	17	*130.1*	9	6	53	49	102	41	17	5	2	0	3.38
95	YANKEES	13	*99*	9	2	42	42	89	47	13	1	0	0	3.82
96	YANKEES	11	72	7	2	25	23	71	34	11	1	0	0	2.88
97	YANKEES	29	195	12	6	67	61	222	86	29	1	0	0	2.82
98	YANKEES	31	207.2	20◆	7	89	82	209	59	31	3	0	0	3.55
MAJ. LEA. TOTALS		359	2396.2	168	93	927	844	2243	895	330	55	21	1	3.17

David had the longest-ever gap between 20-win seasons.

DAVID CONE The well-traveled Cone compiled an amazing list of accomplishments over his 17 seasons in the majors, including five-plus adventurous years with the Yankees. Drafted by his hometown Royals in 1981, Cone was traded to the Mets in '87 and a year later won 20 games. A late-summer 1992 trade sent him to the eventual world champion Blue Jays before he returned to Kansas City, where he won the 1994 Cy Young Award. He landed in the Bronx in time for the Yankees resurgence, winning 64 games and four World Series rings—and pitching a perfect game on July 18, 1999, in a Yankee Stadium interleague contest against Montreal.

Topps card pictured: 1999 #101. Series 2 retail boxes and packs of the 1999 set featured an action photo of Cone's fellow starting pitcher Roger Clemens.

Topps

DAVID CONE

New York Yankees®

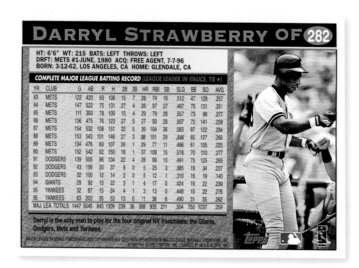

DARRYL STRAWBERRY OF 282

HT: 6'6" WT: 215 BATS: LEFT THROWS: LEFT
DRFT: METS #1-JUNE, 1980 ACQ: FREE AGENT, 7-7-96
BORN: 3-12-62, LOS ANGELES, CA HOME: GLENDALE, CA

COMPLETE MAJOR LEAGUE BATTING RECORD (LEAGUE LEADER IN ITALICS, TIE +)

YR	CLUB	G	AB	R	H	2B	3B	HR	RBI	SB	SLG	BB	SO	AVG
83	METS	122	420	63	108	15	7	26	74	19	.512	47	128	.257
84	METS	147	522	75	131	27	4	26	97	27	.467	75	131	.251
85	METS	111	393	78	109	15	4	29	79	26	.557	73	96	.277
86	METS	136	475	76	123	27	5	27	93	28	.507	72	141	.259
87	METS	154	532	108	151	32	5	39	104	36	.583	97	122	.284
88	METS	153	543	101	146	27	3	39	101	29	.545	85	127	.269
89	METS	134	476	69	107	26	1	29	77	11	.466	61	105	.225
90	METS	152	542	92	150	18	1	37	108	15	.518	70	110	.277
91	DODGERS	139	505	86	134	22	4	28	99	10	.491	75	125	.265
92	DODGERS	43	156	20	37	8	0	5	25	3	.385	19	34	.237
93	DODGERS	32	100	12	14	2	0	5	12	1	.310	16	19	.140
94	GIANTS	29	92	13	22	3	1	4	17	0	.424	19	22	.239
95	YANKEES	32	87	15	24	4	1	3	13	0	.448	10	22	.276
96	YANKEES	63	202	35	53	13	0	11	36	6	.490	31	55	.262
MAJ. LEA. TOTALS		1447	5045	843	1309	239	36	308	935	211	.504	750	1237	.259

Darryl is the only man to play for the four original NY franchises: the Giants, Dodgers, Mets and Yankees.

MAJOR LEAGUE BASEBALL TRADEMARKS AND COPYRIGHTS ARE USED WITH PERMISSION OF MAJOR LEAGUE BASEBALL PROPERTIES, INC. ©1997 THE TOPPS COMPANY INC. | LICENSED BY MLB & MLBPA, 1997

DARRYL STRAWBERRY As a highly touted rookie with the 1983 Mets, Strawberry drew comparisons to Ted Williams because of their similarly sweeping, textbook swings that produced prodigious results, especially towering home runs. The Mets' lanky left-handed slugger summarily engineered a Rookie of the Year campaign featuring 26 homers. Strawberry's arrival also signaled the start of the Mets' steady surge, culminating in an amazin' world championship in 1986. He resurrected a tarnished career when he joined the Yankees in the midst of their 1990s rise, becoming a part-time yet productive contributor to three title teams. In 662 at-bats, Straw hit .255 with 34 doubles, 41 home runs, and 114 RBIs.

Topps card pictured: 1997 #282. Beginning with the 1997 set, Topps retired the use of card #7 in honor of Mickey Mantle and his famous uniform number, which the Yankees retired in 1969.

DARRYLSTRAWBERRY

100

Dwight Gooden
Pitcher

May 14, 1996 (New York) — Dwight "Doc" Gooden not only returned to former glory but, in some sense, surpassed it by firing a no-hitter and defeating the Seattle Mariners, 2-0. It was a career first for the 1985 NL Cy Young Award winner who, a decade ago, was one of the most sensational phenoms in baseball history. An emotional Gooden, who struck out five before an ecstatic crowd of 20,786 at Yankee Stadium, dedicated the gem to his father, who was to undergo surgery the next day.

MAJOR LEAGUE BASEBALL TRADEMARKS AND COPYRIGHTS ARE USED WITH PERMISSION OF MAJOR LEAGUE BASEBALL PROPERTIES, INC.
©1997 THE TOPPS COMPANY, INC. LICENSED BY MLB & MLBPA, 1996

DOC GOODEN In 1984, a year after Darryl Strawberry burst onto the Mets scene and took Rookie of the Year honors, Gooden, just 19, captured the same award with a remarkable 17–9, 2.60 ERA debut, including a league-best 276 strikeouts. Nicknamed Dr. K, he outdid himself in '85, topping the majors in wins (24), strikeouts (268), and ERA (1.53). In the Mets' world championship 1986 season, Doc made his third straight All-Star team and finished 17–6, with 200 strikeouts and a 2.84 ERA. Like Strawberry, Gooden unfortunately fell from grace, then enjoyed a resurgence with the Yankees during their 1990s prime—highlighted by a no-hitter on May 14, 1996, versus the Mariners.

Topps card pictured: 1997 #100. In honor of his 1996 selection as the AL's top newcomer, Topps randomly inserted a special "Derek Jeter Rookie of the Year" autographed card in the 1997 Series 2 packs.

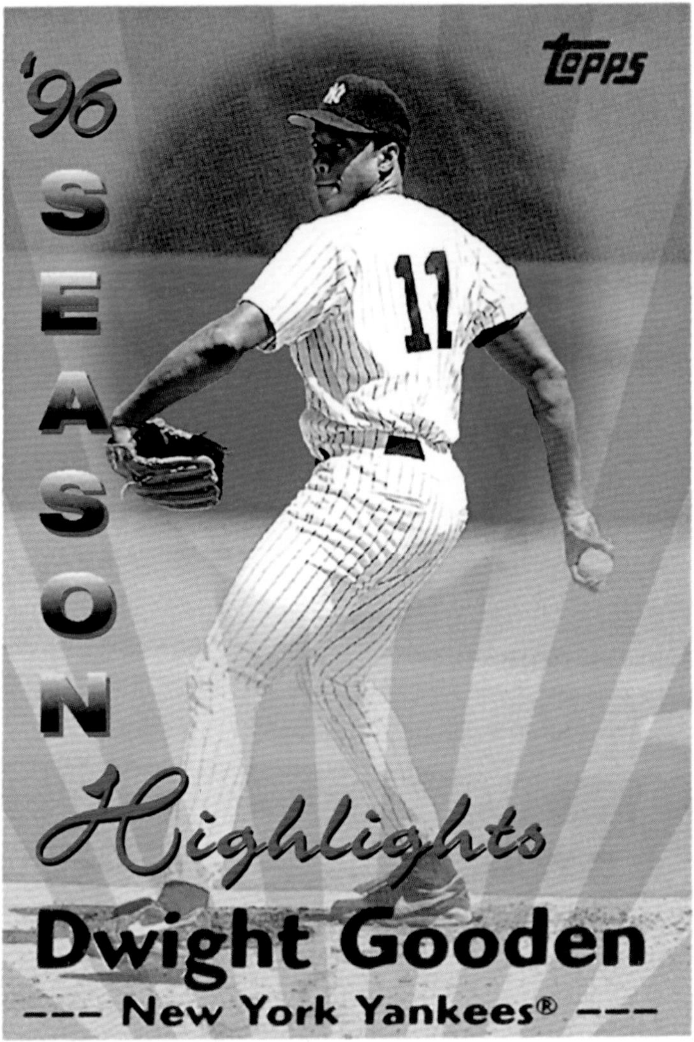
Topps
'96
SEASON
Highlights
Dwight Gooden
--- New York Yankees® ---

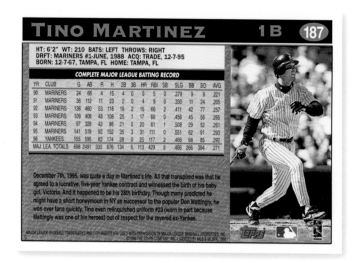

TINO MARTINEZ — 1B — 187

HT: 6'2" WT: 210 BATS: LEFT THROWS: RIGHT
DRFT: MARINERS #1-JUNE, 1988 ACQ: TRADE, 12-7-95
BORN: 12-7-67, TAMPA, FL HOME: TAMPA, FL

COMPLETE MAJOR LEAGUE BATTING RECORD

YR	CLUB	G	AB	R	H	2B	3B	HR	RBI	SB	SLG	BB	SO	AVG
90	MARINERS	24	68	4	15	4	0	0	5	0	.279	9	9	.221
91	MARINERS	36	112	11	23	2	0	4	9	0	.330	11	24	.205
92	MARINERS	136	460	53	118	19	2	16	66	2	.411	42	77	.257
93	MARINERS	109	408	48	108	25	1	17	60	0	.456	45	56	.265
94	MARINERS	97	329	42	86	21	0	20	61	1	.508	29	52	.261
95	MARINERS	141	519	92	152	35	3	31	111	0	.551	62	91	.293
96	YANKEES	155	595	82	174	28	0	25	117	2	.466	68	85	.292
	MAJ LEA TOTALS	698	2491	332	676	134	6	113	429	5	.466	266	394	.271

December 7th, 1995, was quite a day in Martinez's life. All that transpired was that he agreed to a lucrative, five-year Yankee contract and witnessed the birth of his baby girl, Victoria. And it happened to be his 28th birthday. Though many predicted he might have a short honeymoon in NY as successor to the popular Don Mattingly, he won over fans quickly. Tino even relinquished uniform #23 (worn in part because Mattingly was one of his heroes) out of respect for the revered ex-Yankee.

TINO MARTINEZ The trade that brought Martinez to New York from Seattle for the 1996 season coincided with a rebirth of the Yankees and the beginning of their remarkable run of four World Series titles in five years. A rock at first base, he was a pillar at the plate, too, averaging 161 hits, 30 doubles, 29 home runs, and 115 RBIs over his six-year stint in the Bronx (he returned in 2005 for his MLB finale). "The Bamtino," as Yankees radio announcer John Sterling dubbed him, will forever be revered for his go-ahead Game 1 grand slam that powered the Yanks to a sweep of the Padres in the 1998 Series.

Topps card pictured: 1997 #187. In 1977, Topps included a special Jackie Robinson card, #42 (his uniform number, which every team retired in 1987), to mark the 50th anniversary of his historic MLB debut.

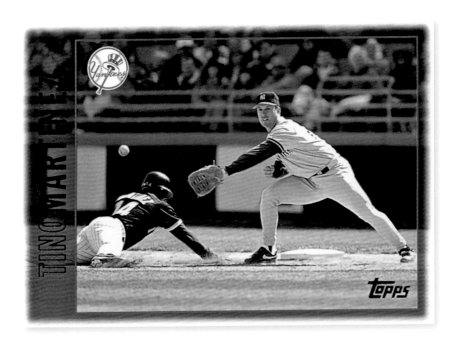

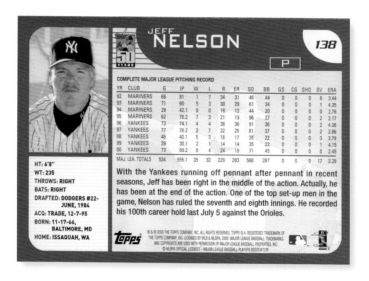

JEFF **NELSON** 138

P

COMPLETE MAJOR LEAGUE PITCHING RECORD

YR	CLUB	G	IP	W	L	R	ER	SO	BB	GS	CG	SHO	SV	ERA
92	MARINERS	66	81	1	7	34	31	46	44	0	0	0	6	3.44
93	MARINERS	71	60	5	3	30	29	61	34	0	0	0	1	4.35
94	MARINERS	28	42.1	0	0	18	13	44	20	0	0	0	0	2.76
95	MARINERS	62	78.2	7	3	21	19	96	27	0	0	0	2	2.17
96	YANKEES	73	74.1	4	4	38	36	91	36	0	0	0	2	4.36
97	YANKEES	77	78.2	3	7	32	25	81	37	0	0	0	2	2.86
98	YANKEES	45	40.1	5	3	18	17	35	22	0	0	0	3	3.79
99	YANKEES	39	30.1	2	1	14	14	35	22	0	0	0	1	4.15
00	YANKEES	73	69.2	8	4	24	19	71	45	0	0	0	0	2.45
MAJ. LEA. TOTALS		534	555.1	35	32	229	203	560	287	0	0	0	17	3.29

HT: 6'8"
WT: 235
THROWS: RIGHT
BATS: RIGHT
DRAFTED: DODGERS #22-
    JUNE, 1984
ACQ: TRADE, 12-7-95
BORN: 11-17-66,
    BALTIMORE, MD
HOME: ISSAQUAH, WA

With the Yankees running off pennant after pennant in recent seasons, Jeff has been right in the middle of the action. Actually, he has been at the end of the action. One of the top set-up men in the game, Nelson has ruled the seventh and eighth innings. He recorded his 100th career hold last July 5 against the Orioles.

® & © 2000 THE TOPPS COMPANY, INC. ALL RIGHTS RESERVED. TOPPS IS A REGISTERED TRADEMARK OF THE TOPPS COMPANY, INC. LICENSED BY MLB & MLBPA, 2000. MAJOR LEAGUE BASEBALL TRADEMARKS AND COPYRIGHTS ARE USED WITH PERMISSION OF MAJOR LEAGUE BASEBALL PROPERTIES, INC.
© MLBPA OFFICIAL LICENSEE · MAJOR LEAGUE BASEBALL PLAYERS ASSOCIATION

JEFF NELSON   Much of the success of the Yankees dynasty that won four World Series in five years from 1996 to 2000 can be attributed to one of the best bullpens ever. Of course, most every reliever was setting up closer extraordinaire Mariano Rivera, and Nellie was a resilient righty, appearing in 307 regular-season games while compiling a 3.41 ERA with 313 strikeouts. He threw his signature "Frisbee" curveball, which devastated right-handed batters, in 13 postseason series for the Yanks, of which they lost only one. In the postseason during New York's five-AL-pennant run, Nelson held righties to a measly .118 batting average.

Topps card pictured: 2001 #138. Celebrating Topps 50th anniversary in the baseball card business, the 2001 set contained randomly inserted original cards from past years, as well as cards autographed by past and current stars, including Whitey Ford and Reggie Jackson.

Jeff **NELSON**

MIKE STANTON Beginning in 1997, the Yankees, and their deflated opponents, quickly learned that getting to Mariano Rivera in tight ball games was imperative. With a lead, however slim, they'd go to Mo for the save. That put a heavy burden, however, on his set-up men, and from the left side, Mike Stanton became the man. Combining a crackling fastball with a wicked curve to rack up strikeouts, he teamed with right-hander Jeff Nelson to give the Yanks a potent one-two jab leading to Rivera's knockout punch. Stanton excelled in New York's three world championships from 1998 to 2000, posting the lowest-ever ERA among relievers.

Topps card pictured: 2000 #324. In 2000, to mark the new millennium, Topps randomly inserted 10 relic cards featuring not only photos of star players but also actual tiny pieces (mostly bases) of their home stadiums. Don Mattingly (#SR1) represented the Yankees and the House That Ruth Built.

TOPPS 2000

MIKE STANTON

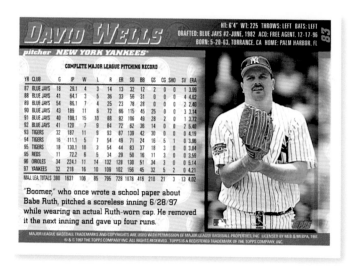

DAVID WELLS
HT: 6'4" WT: 225 THROWS: LEFT BATS: LEFT
DRAFTED: BLUE JAYS #2-JUNE, 1982 ACQ: FREE AGENT, 12-17-96
BORN: 5-20-63, TORRANCE, CA HOME: PALM HARBOR, FL

83

pitcher *NEW YORK YANKEES*

COMPLETE MAJOR LEAGUE PITCHING RECORD

YR	CLUB	G	IP	W	L	R	ER	SO	BB	GS	CG	SHO	SV	ERA
87	BLUE JAYS	18	29.1	4	3	14	13	32	12	2	0	0	1	3.99
88	BLUE JAYS	41	64.1	3	5	36	33	56	31	0	0	0	4	4.62
89	BLUE JAYS	54	86.1	7	4	25	23	78	28	0	0	0	2	2.40
90	BLUE JAYS	43	189	11	6	72	66	115	45	25	0	0	3	3.14
91	BLUE JAYS	40	198.1	15	10	88	82	106	49	28	2	0	1	3.72
92	BLUE JAYS	41	120	7	9	84	72	62	36	14	0	0	2	5.40
93	TIGERS	32	187	11	9	93	87	139	42	30	0	0	0	4.19
94	TIGERS	16	111.1	5	7	54	49	71	24	16	5	1	0	3.96
95	TIGERS	18	130.1	10	3	54	44	83	37	18	3	0	0	3.04
95	REDS	11	72.2	6	5	34	29	50	16	11	3	0	0	3.59
96	ORIOLES	34	224.1	11	14	132	128	130	51	34	3	0	0	5.14
97	YANKEES	32	218	16	10	109	102	156	45	32	5	2	0	4.21
MAJ. LEA. TOTALS		380	1631	106	85	795	728	1078	416	210	21	3	13	4.02

"Boomer," who once wrote a school paper about Babe Ruth, pitched a scoreless inning 6/28/97 while wearing an actual Ruth-worn cap. He removed it the next inning and gave up four runs.

DAVID WELLS   A reliever turned starter with the two-time world champion Blue Jays, Wells spent time in Detroit, Cincinnati, and Baltimore before signing with New York as a free agent in 1997. Following a 16–10 campaign, the hefty lefty led the staff with 18 victories in the Yanks' 1998 record-breaking 114-win dream season. In the ALCS, his 2–0 record garnered him MVP honors. Then, in the World Series, Boomer won Game 1 in the sweep of the Padres. The '98 season, and Wells's career, were highlighted by the perfect game he twirled against the Twins at Yankee Stadium on May 17.

Topps card pictured: 1998 #83. The 1998 set includes a special subset commemorating the Hall of Fame career of Pittsburgh Pirates great Roberto Clemente.

DAVID WELLS
NEW YORK YANKEES

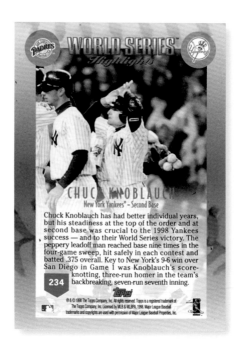

CHUCK KNOBLAUCH From his 1991 Rookie of the Year season in Minnesota, Knoblauch developed into an All-Star, Gold Glove second baseman with a productive bat and a passion for base thievery. In the postseason leading to Minnesota's '91 world championship, he hit .326 with five RBIs and six steals. He added power to his repertoire when traded to New York in 1998, contributing 17 homers to the Yankees juggernaut that won a record 114 games in the regular season. In Game 1 of the World Series against the Padres, Knoblauch smacked a game-tying homer that set the tone for a sweep and the first of three straight titles.

Topps card pictured: 1999 #234. The 1999 set included randomly inserted reprints of Nolan Ryan cards from 1968 to 1994, commemorating the fireballer's Hall of Fame induction in '99.

WORLD SERIES '98

CHUCK KNOBLAUCH

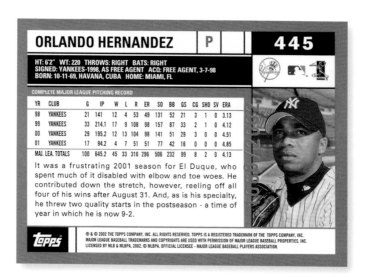

ORLANDO HERNANDEZ   **P**   **445**

HT: 6'2" WT: 220 THROWS: RIGHT BATS: RIGHT
SIGNED: YANKEES-1998, AS FREE AGENT ACQ: FREE AGENT, 3-7-98
BORN: 10-11-69, HAVANA, CUBA HOME: MIAMI, FL

COMPLETE MAJOR LEAGUE PITCHING RECORD

YR	CLUB	G	IP	W	L	R	ER	SO	BB	GS	CG	SHO	SV	ERA
98	YANKEES	21	141	12	4	53	49	131	52	21	3	1	0	3.13
99	YANKEES	33	214.1	17	9	108	98	157	87	33	2	1	0	4.12
00	YANKEES	29	195.2	12	13	104	98	141	51	29	3	0	0	4.51
01	YANKEES	17	94.2	4	7	51	51	77	42	16	0	0	0	4.85
MAJ. LEA. TOTALS		100	645.2	45	33	316	296	506	232	99	8	2	0	4.13

It was a frustrating 2001 season for El Duque, who spent much of it disabled with elbow and toe woes. He contributed down the stretch, however, reeling off all four of his wins after August 31. And, as is his specialty, he threw two quality starts in the postseason - a time of year in which he is now 9-2.

ORLANDO HERNANDEZ   Already a veteran star in Cuba, whose communist regime wouldn't allow its players to join MLB, Hernandez made a daring defection in 1998 and became a free agent signed by the Yankees. With his derring-do backstory and balletic windup, featuring an exaggerated leg kick, El Duque fit perfectly in New York and in a rotation that paced the club to its historic 114-win season and dominant postseason march to the world championship. Keeping his cool under pressure in those and five other playoff series, Hernandez became the first pitcher in baseball history to win his first eight postseason decisions.

Topps card pictured: 2002 #445. The '99 set included randomly inserted cards autographed by Hall of Famers including Whitey Ford, Willie Mays, and Robin Roberts.

2002 TOPPS
51 YEARS OF COLLECTING

ORLANDO HERNANDEZ

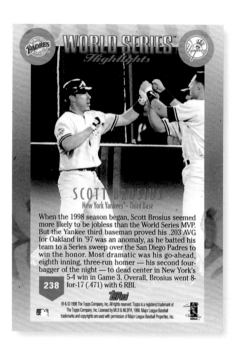

SCOTT BROSIUS Brosius had an erratic career with Oakland, but enough
upside to convince the Yankees he could handle the third-base job in 1998. He
did that, and much more, putting together an All-Star year capped off with a
phenomenal postseason. Brosius hit .300 with 19 homers and a personal-best
98 RBIs while the Yankees amassed 114 wins, the most in AL history. After hitting a combined .333 with 9 RBIs in the AL divisional and championship series,
he went 8 for 17 with 2 home runs and 6 RBIs in the World Series sweep of the
Padres—plenty to earn Series MVP honors.

Topps card pictured: 1999 #238. While this card celebrates Brosius's MVP performance in the 1998 World
Series win over the Padres, he was no slouch in the '99 Series sweep of the Braves, hitting .375 and flash-
ing the skills at third base that earned him a Gold Glove that season.

WORLD SERIES

'98

SCOTT BROSIUS

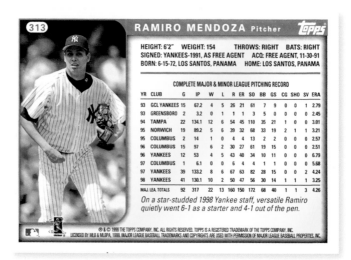

RAMIRO MENDOZA Pitcher

HEIGHT: 6'2"   WEIGHT: 154   THROWS: RIGHT   BATS: RIGHT
SIGNED: YANKEES-1991, AS FREE AGENT   ACQ: FREE AGENT, 11-30-91
BORN: 6-15-72, LOS SANTOS, PANAMA   HOME: LOS SANTOS, PANAMA

COMPLETE MAJOR & MINOR LEAGUE PITCHING RECORD

YR	CLUB	G	IP	W	L	R	ER	SO	BB	GS	CG	SHO	SV	ERA
93	GCL YANKEES	15	67.2	4	5	26	21	61	7	9	0	0	1	2.79
93	GREENSBORO	2	3.2	0	1	1	1	3	5	0	0	0	0	2.45
94	TAMPA	22	134.1	12	6	54	45	110	35	21	1	0	0	3.01
95	NORWICH	19	89.2	5	6	39	32	68	33	19	2	1	1	3.21
95	COLUMBUS	2	14	1	0	4	4	13	2	2	0	0	0	2.57
96	COLUMBUS	15	97	6	2	30	27	61	19	15	0	0	0	2.51
96	YANKEES	12	53	4	5	43	40	34	10	11	0	0	0	6.79
97	COLUMBUS	1	6.1	0	0	6	4	4	1	1	0	0	0	5.68
97	YANKEES	39	133.2	8	6	67	63	82	28	15	0	0	2	4.24
98	YANKEES	41	130.1	10	2	50	47	56	30	14	1	1	1	3.25
MAJ. LEA. TOTALS		92	317	22	13	160	150	172	68	40	1	1	3	4.26

*On a star-studded 1998 Yankee staff, versatile Ramiro
quietly went 6-1 as a starter and 4-1 out of the pen.*

RAMIRO MENDOZA   Middle relievers usually don't get as much fan and media attention as ace starters or lock-down closers. Yet ones as indispensable as Mendoza was to the Yankees staff during their historic run in the 1990s get plenty of notice. The tall, slender Panamanian with the deadly sinker and filthy slider was a mainstay in the bullpen, routinely called on to get groundball outs—and the Yanks out of many a jam. Also an emergency starter, Mendoza was a big part of four world championship teams, and was usually coveted by other clubs whenever trades were discussed.

Topps card pictured: 1999 #313. As indispensable as Mendoza was during his regular season appearances, his relief work in four AL Championship Series proved pivotal. Over 14 innings he gave up only nine hits, issued one walk, and struck out seven batters while compiling a stunning 1.29 ERA.

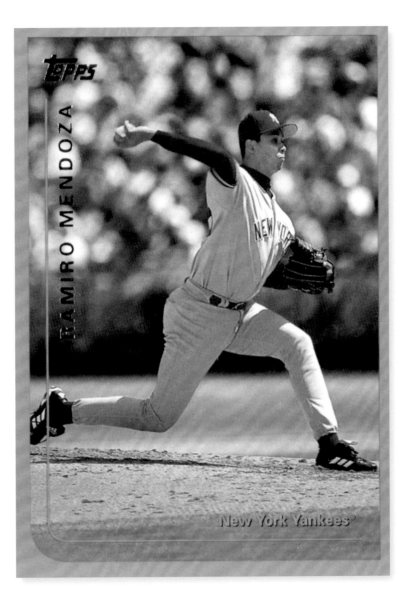

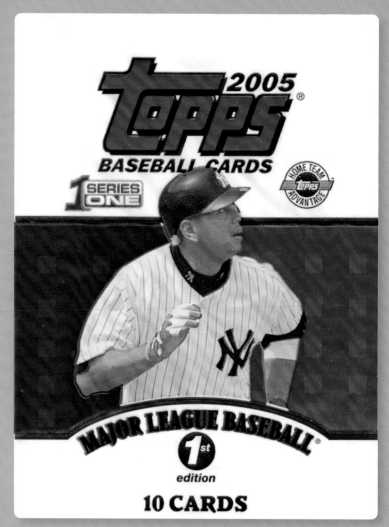

2005 foil pack for Series 1, 1st Edition cards

PART 6 · 2000s

The greatest baseball team of the 20th century ushered in the 21st in traditional fashion—with another World Series title. The win marked baseball's first "threepeat" since the Oakland Athletics did it from 1972 to '74. Plus, it was New York City's first Subway Series in 44 years, dating back to 1956, when the Bronx Bombers bested Brooklyn's Dodgers in seven games. Against the Mets, the "Core Four" homegrown Yanks—Jeter, Posada, Pettitte, and Rivera—remained the heart of the team. Some new additions pitched in, too. Roger Clemens, in particular, finally added a World Series ring to his awards hardware after the Yankees prevailed in five games.

In 2001, Clemens won 16 straight games on his way to becoming the first pitcher to earn six Cy Young Awards. He was joined in the rotation by Mike Mussina, the former Orioles ace, who, on September 2 versus Boston, came within a strike of pitching a perfect game. Only days later, the Yanks' road to the postseason was tragically interrupted by the September 11 terrorist attacks, and it seemed only fitting that a team from New York, where the World Trade Center's twin towers were destroyed, would play in the World Series. While the Bombers lifted the city's spirits with two unbelievable walk-off victories against the Diamondbacks in Games 4 and 5, a rare misstep by Mariano Rivera and a bloop single by Luis Gonzalez in the bottom of the ninth of Game 7 gave the Arizona expansion team its first championship.

The Yankees reign over the AL East continued through 2006, and they made it back to the World Series in '03, only to fall to another expansion team, the Florida Marlins. It was their old nemesis in Boston, however, that left the biggest blemish on the Yanks' incredible playoffs record. In the 2004 ALCS, the Red Sox became baseball's first team ever to come back from an 0–3 deficit in postseason play. The Yankees' loss to the Indians in the 2007 Division Series, as the AL's wild card entry, also marked the end of the Joe Torre era. Under successor Joe Girardi in '08, the team's string of 13 straight playoff appearances was snapped, though they rebounded in typical Yankees fashion in '09, winning the franchise's 27th world championship by topping the Phillies in six games.

The new millennium brought continued success for Topps as well. The company continued to treat collectors to a series of innovations, including the Heritage set, eTopps, relic cards, and the 10-card Mantle Collection, with each card designed after a Topps set from 1996 to 2005. The decade ended with the announcement that Topps had been designated by MLB to be its exclusive, official card producer beginning in 2010. Appropriately, that year coincided with the company's 60th Diamond Anniversary, which it celebrated by releasing special, limited-edition, diamond-embedded and diamond die-cut hologram cards, and by offering collectors a chance to win actual his and hers diamond rings.

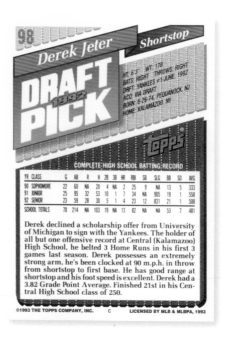

DEREK JETER In 1992, the Yankees wanted to make Jeter's boyhood dream of playing shortstop for his favorite team come true, but feared he might accept a college scholarship. "The only place Derek Jeter's going," scout Dick Groch assured them, "is to Cooperstown." Nearly two decades later, Jeter guaranteed that prophecy with his 3,000th hit—a home run, no less—though he already had a Hall of Fame–worthy résumé. Aside from holding the MLB record for most career hits by a shortstop, the Yankees captain owns a slew of team records, and his non-statistical intangibles remain legend. Jeter's shined brightest in seven World Series, with 50 hits, a .321 batting average, and an .832 OPS.

Topps card pictured: 1993 #98. Jeter's Topps rookie card got a boost in value on July 9, 2011, when he became the 28th major leaguer—and first Yankee—to reach 3,000 career hits.

1992 DRAFT PICK

DEREK JETER

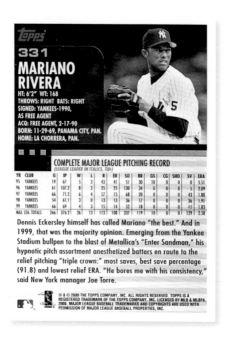

MARIANO RIVERA "Incomparable" often precedes his name, and that perfectly describes Mariano Rivera, the greatest relief pitcher in baseball history. He came up to the majors as a starter in 1995, moved to the bullpen as the setup man for closer John Wetteland in '96, then assumed the closer role in '97. Since then, using basically one pitch—a bat-shattering, heartbreaking cut fastball that baffles batters—Mo has accumulated unmatched regular-season numbers. On September 19, 2011, he broke Trevor Hoffman's record for most career saves (601). Rivera's been incomparably great in 15 postseason series (a 0.71 ERA in 94 appearances), 5 of which culminated in World Series championships.

Topps card pictured: 2000 #331. In addition to this card, the 2000 set also featured Rivera on an "Own the Game" card (#OTG24) and a special card (#228) marking the Yankees' 1999 World Series sweep of the Braves, in which Mo's 4.2 scoreless innings and two saves earned him the MVP Award.

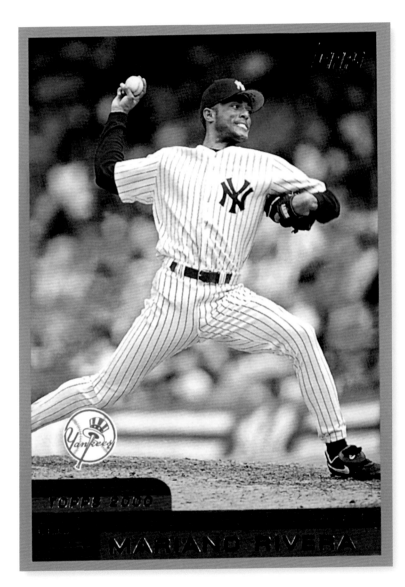

TOPPS 2000

MARIANO RIVERA

418

ANDY PETTITTE
NEW YORK YANKEES

Lyle Overbay .166 • Jason Tyner .316 • Cristian Guzman .327 • Akinora Iwamura .360 • Ty Wigginton .372 • Aubrey Huff .391 (active batters, min. 20 PAs)

HT: 6'5" WT: 225 THROWS: LEFT BATS: LEFT DRAFTED: YANKEES #22-JUNE, 1991
ACQ: FREE AGENT, 12-8-06 BORN: 6-15-72, BATON ROUGE, LA HOME: DEER PARK, TX

COMPLETE MAJOR LEAGUE PITCHING RECORD

YR	CLUB	G	IP	W	L	R	ER	SO	BB	GS	CG	SHO	SV	WHIP	ERA
95	YANKEES	31	175	12	9	86	81	114	63	26	3	0	0	1.41	4.17
96	YANKEES	35	221	21	8	105	95	162	72	34	2	0	0	1.36	3.87
97	YANKEES	35	240.1	18	7	86	77	166	65	35◆	4	1	0	1.24	2.88
98	YANKEES	33	216.1	16	11	110	102	146	87	32	5	0	0	1.45	4.24
99	YANKEES	31	191.2	14	11	105	100	121	89	31	0	0	0	1.59	4.70
00	YANKEES	32	204.2	19	9	111	99	125	80	32	3	1	0	1.46	4.35
01	YANKEES	31	200.2	15	10	103	89	164	41	31	2	0	0	1.32	3.99
02	YANKEES	22	134.2	13	5	58	49	97	32	22	3	1	0	1.31	3.27
03	YANKEES	33	208.1	21	8	109	93	180	50	33	1	0	0	1.33	4.02
04	ASTROS	15	83	6	4	37	36	79	31	15	0	0	0	1.23	3.90
05	ASTROS	33	222.1	17	9	66	59	171	41	33	0	0	0	1.03	2.39
06	ASTROS	36	214.1	14	13	114	100	178	7	35◆	0	0	0	1.44	4.20
07	YANKEES	36	215.1	15	9	106	97	141	69	34◆	0	0	0	1.43	4.05
08	YANKEES	33	204	14	14	112	103	158	55	33	0	0	0	1.41	4.54
	MAJ. LEA. TOTALS	436	2731.2	215	127	1308	1180	2002	845	426	25	4	0	1.36	3.89

ANDY PETTITTE Pettitte epitomizes Yankees pride: toughness, perseverance, and an unwavering desire to win. Over his 13 seasons in pinstripes—interrupted by a stint with the Astros from 2004 to 2006—he faithfully toed the rubber every five days. Even if he didn't have his best stuff, he powered on, averaging a Herculean 215 innings pitched over his career. In 1996, he won an AL-best 21 games, and in the pivotal Game 5 of the World Series versus Atlanta, he outdueled John Smoltz in a 1–0 victory. During the playoffs of his penultimate 2009 campaign, Pettitte won all three series-clinching games, finishing his outstanding career as the all-time leader in postseason victories, with 19.

Topps card pictured: 2009 #418. Retail boxes and packs of the '09 Series 1 set featured photos of Yankees greats Alex Rodriguez and Babe Ruth.

Topps

YANKEES

P

ANDY PETTITTE

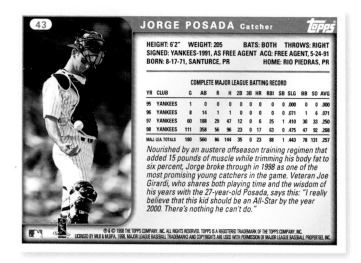

JORGE POSADA   Posada was old school. Not that other veterans didn't play with his hard-nosed style, but Jorge did it in the Yankees tradition. He came up through the farm system with Derek Jeter, Mariano Rivera, and Andy Pettitte, and the so-called Core Four won five World Series from 1996 to 2009. Before wear and tear moved him to the designated hitter role in 2011, Jorge was a perennial force behind the plate. And like many previous Yankees catchers (Dickey, Berra, Howard, Munson), he swung a mighty bat, too. From 2000 to '10, the age-defying switch-hitter had more runs batted in, home runs, and hits than any other catcher in baseball. He retired, at 40, in January 2012.

Topps card pictured: 1999 #43. On the back of Posada's 1999 card, former teammate and eventual manager Joe Girardi predicts Posada will be an All-Star by 2000, which was indeed his first of five trips to the Midsummer Classic.

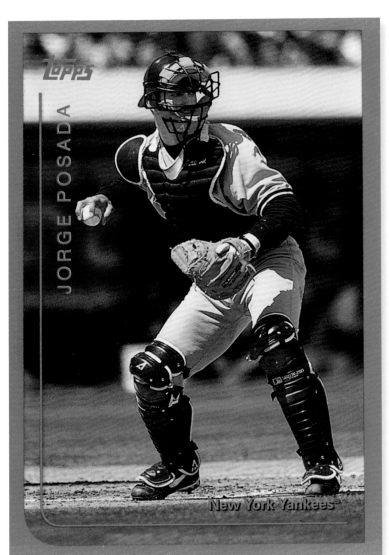

JORGE POSADA

New York Yankees®

ALFONSO SORIANO Soriano was a phenom with the Yankees before becoming part of the blockbuster deal that brought Alex Rodriguez to the Bronx in 2004. Soriano signed with the Yanks in 1998 and spent most of the next two years in the minors. Fans caught a glimpse of greatness during a September '99 call-up. It came on Soriano's first big-league hit, an 11th-inning walk-off homer to beat the Rays. After a solid rookie season in 2001, in '02 he paced the AL in runs (128), hits (209), and steals (41), and his 39 homers left him just shy of becoming MLB's first 40-40 second baseman.

Topps card pictured: 2003 #357. Series 1 of the 2003 set included randomly inserted Soriano cards featuring his authentic autograph.

Topps

The Sporting News
All-Stars

AMERICAN LEAGUE

2B

ALFONSO SORIANO

ROGER CLEMENS P

105

HT: 6'4" WT: 235
THROWS: RIGHT
BATS: RIGHT

●●●●● **NEW YORK YANKEES®** ●●●●●

DRAFTED: RED SOX #1-JUNE, 1983   ACQ: FREE AGENT, 5-6-07

BORN: 8-4-62,
DAYTON,
OHIO

COMPLETE MAJOR LEAGUE PITCHING RECORD *LEAGUE LEADER IN ITALICS, TIE ◆*

YR CLUB	G	IP	W	L	R	ER	SO	BB	GS	CG	SHO	SV	WHIP	ERA
84 RED SOX	21	133.1	9	4	67	64	126	29	20	5	1	0	1.31	4.32
85 RED SOX	15	98.1	7	5	38	36	74	37	15	3	1	0	1.22	3.29
86 RED SOX	33	254	*24*	4	77	70	238	67	33	10	1	0	*0.97*	*2.48*
87 RED SOX	36	281.2	*20◆*	9	100	93	256	83	36	*18*	*7*	0	1.18	2.97
88 RED SOX	35	264	18	12	93	86	*291*	62	35	*14◆*	*8*	0	1.06	2.93
89 RED SOX	35	253.1	17	11	101	88	230	93	35	8	3	0	1.22	3.13
90 RED SOX	31	228.1	21	6	59	49	209	54	31	7	*4◆*	0	1.08	*1.93*
91 RED SOX	35	*271.1*	18	10	93	79	*241*	65	*35◆*	13	*4*	0	1.05	*2.62*
92 RED SOX	32	246.2	18	11	80	66	208	62	32	11	*5*	0	*1.07*	*2.41*
93 RED SOX	29	191.2	11	14	99	95	160	67	29	2	1	0	1.26	4.46
94 RED SOX	24	170.2	9	7	62	54	168	71	24	3	1	0	1.14	2.85
95 RED SOX	23	140	10	5	70	65	132	60	23	0	0	0	1.44	4.18
96 RED SOX	34	242.2	10	13	106	98	*257*	106	34	6	2	0	1.33	3.63
97 BLUE JAYS	34	*264* ◆	*21*	7	65	60	*292*	68	34	*9◆*	*3◆*	0	*1.03*	*2.05*
98 BLUE JAYS	33	234.2	*20◆*	6	78	69	*271*	88	33	5	3	0	1.10	*2.65*
99 YANKEES	30	187.2	14	10	101	96	163	90	30	1	1	0	1.47	4.60
00 YANKEES	32	204.1	13	8	96	84	188	84	32	1	0	0	1.31	3.70
01 YANKEES	33	220.1	20	3	94	86	213	72	32	0	0	0	1.26	3.51
02 YANKEES	29	180	13	6	94	87	192	63	29	0	0	0	1.31	4.35
03 YANKEES	33	211.2	17	9	99	92	190	58	33	1	0	0	1.21	3.91
04 ASTROS	33	214.1	18	4	76	71	218	79	33	0	0	0	1.16	2.98
05 ASTROS	32	211.1	13	8	51	44	185	62	32	1	0	0	1.01	*1.87*
06 ASTROS	19	113.1	7	6	34	29	102	29	19	0	0	0	1.04	2.30
07 YANKEES	18	99	6	6	52	46	68	31	17	0	0	0	1.31	4.18
MAJ. LEA. TOTALS	**709**	**4916.2**	**354**	**184**	**1885**	**1707**	**4672**	**1580**	**707**	**118**	**46**	**0**	**1.17**	**3.12**

® ↓ © 2008 THE TOPPS COMPANY, INC. ALL RIGHTS RESERVED. TOPPS IS A REGISTERED TRADEMARK OF THE TOPPS COMPANY, INC. MAJOR LEAGUE BASEBALL TRADEMARKS AND COPYRIGHTS ARE USED WITH PERMISSION OF MAJOR LEAGUE BASEBALL PROPERTIES, INC. LICENSED BY MLBP & MLBPA, 2008. © MLBPA. OFFICIAL LICENSEE – MAJOR LEAGUE BASEBALL PLAYERS ASSOCIATION. MLB.COM

ROGER CLEMENS   One of baseball's greatest right-handers ever, Clemens dominated batters throughout his phenomenal 1986 season with the Red Sox, pacing the AL in wins (24) and ERA (2.48) to lock up both the Cy Young and MVP awards. He repeated as the league's best pitcher again in '87 and '91. The Rocket led the league in ERA three years in a row (1990–'92) and piled up 2,590 strikeouts during his 13 seasons in Boston. After back-to-back Cy Young Award–winning seasons in Toronto, he was traded to New York in 1999, where he won yet another Cy Young, going 20–3 in 2001, and two World Series.

Topps card pictured: 2008 #105. Although the Rocket was featured on this and several "Moments & Milestones" cards in 2008, he had actually finished his stellar career in '07.

YANKEES

Topps

ROGER CLEMENS

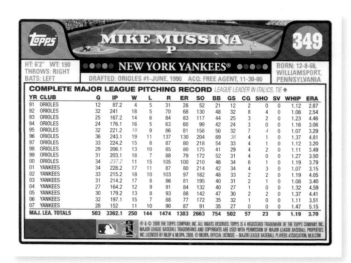

MIKE MUSSINA — P

NEW YORK YANKEES®

HT: 6'2" WT: 190
THROWS: RIGHT
BATS: LEFT

BORN: 12-8-68,
WILLIAMSPORT,
PENNSYLVANIA

DRAFTED: ORIOLES #1-JUNE, 1990   ACQ: FREE AGENT, 11-30-00

COMPLETE MAJOR LEAGUE PITCHING RECORD *LEAGUE LEADER IN ITALICS, TIE ◆*

YR	CLUB	G	IP	W	L	R	ER	SO	BB	GS	CG	SHO	SV	WHIP	ERA
91	ORIOLES	12	87.2	4	5	31	28	52	21	12	2	0	0	1.12	2.87
92	ORIOLES	32	241	18	5	70	68	130	48	32	8	4	0	1.08	2.54
93	ORIOLES	25	167.2	14	6	84	83	117	44	25	3	2	0	1.23	4.46
94	ORIOLES	24	176.1	16	5	63	60	99	42	24	3	0	0	1.16	3.06
95	ORIOLES	32	221.2	*19*	9	86	81	158	50	32	7	*4*	0	1.07	3.29
96	ORIOLES	36	243.1	19	11	137	130	204	69	*36*	4	1	0	1.37	4.81
97	ORIOLES	33	224.2	15	8	87	80	218	54	33	4	1	0	1.12	3.20
98	ORIOLES	29	206.1	13	10	85	80	175	41	29	4	2	0	1.11	3.49
99	ORIOLES	31	203.1	18	7	88	79	172	52	31	4	0	0	1.27	3.50
00	ORIOLES	34	*237.2*	11	15	105	100	210	46	34	6	1	0	1.19	3.79
01	YANKEES	34	228.2	17	11	87	80	214	42	34	4	3	0	1.07	3.15
02	YANKEES	33	215.2	18	10	103	97	182	48	33	2	2	0	1.19	4.05
03	YANKEES	31	214.2	17	8	86	81	195	40	31	2	1	0	1.08	3.40
04	YANKEES	27	164.2	12	9	91	84	132	40	27	1	0	0	1.32	4.59
05	YANKEES	30	179.2	13	8	93	88	142	47	30	2	2	0	1.37	4.41
06	YANKEES	32	197.1	15	7	88	77	172	35	32	1	0	0	1.11	3.51
07	YANKEES	28	152	11	10	90	87	91	35	27	0	0	0	1.47	5.15
MAJ. LEA. TOTALS		**503**	**3362.1**	**250**	**144**	**1474**	**1383**	**2663**	**754**	**502**	**57**	**23**	**0**	**1.19**	**3.70**

MIKE MUSSINA   Over his career, Mussina pitched back-to-back 19-win seasons and three times won 18 games, but it wasn't until his 18th and final season that he finished with 20 victories. Moose also twice came within one or two outs of throwing a no-hitter, and although he appeared in five AL Championship Series and two World Series, he never won it all. It adds up to, in many observers' minds, a Hall of Fame career, though that remains an achievement-in-waiting. During eight years in pinstripes, Mussina was rock solid, averaging almost 200 innings pitched and 160 shutouts and finishing with an excellent 123–72 record and a 3.88 ERA.

Topps card pictured: 2008 #349. In 2008, Topps featured Year in Review cards chronicling great moments in 2007. Moose is recalled (#YR131) for his August 11 win against Cleveland, which made him the 16th Yankees hurler to reach the century mark.

YANKEES

MIKE MUSSINA

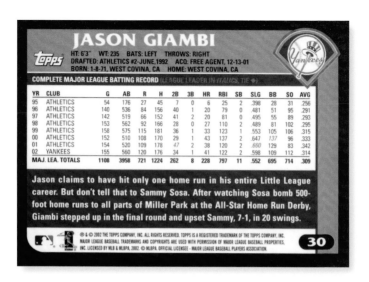

JASON GIAMBI

HT: 6'3" WT: 235 BATS: LEFT THROWS: RIGHT
DRAFTED: ATHLETICS #2-JUNE,1992 ACQ: FREE AGENT, 12-13-01
BORN: 1-8-71, WEST COVINA, CA HOME: WEST COVINA, CA

COMPLETE MAJOR LEAGUE BATTING RECORD (LEAGUE LEADER IN ITALICS, TIE ♦)

YR	CLUB	G	AB	R	H	2B	3B	HR	RBI	SB	SLG	BB	SO	AVG
95	ATHLETICS	54	176	27	45	7	0	6	25	2	.398	28	31	.256
96	ATHLETICS	140	536	84	156	40	1	20	79	0	.481	51	95	.291
97	ATHLETICS	142	519	66	152	41	2	20	81	0	.495	55	89	.293
98	ATHLETICS	153	562	92	166	28	0	27	110	2	.489	81	102	.295
99	ATHLETICS	158	575	115	181	36	1	33	123	1	.553	105	106	.315
00	ATHLETICS	152	510	108	170	29	1	43	137	2	.647	*137*	96	.333
01	ATHLETICS	154	520	109	178	47	2	38	120	2	*.660*	129	83	.342
02	YANKEES	155	560	120	176	34	1	41	122	2	.598	109	112	.314
MAJ. LEA. TOTALS		**1108**	**3958**	**721**	**1224**	**262**	**8**	**228**	**797**	**11**	**.552**	**695**	**714**	**.309**

Jason claims to have hit only one home run in his entire Little League
career. But don't tell that to Sammy Sosa. After watching Sosa bomb 500-
foot home runs to all parts of Miller Park at the All-Star Home Run Derby,
Giambi stepped up in the final round and upset Sammy, 7-1, in 20 swings.

30

JASON GIAMBI Giambi arrived in New York in 2002 with a powerful
résumé: MVP Award; two-time All-Star; 187 home runs, 675 RBIs, and a .308
batting average in seven years with the A's. Yankees fans embraced the fun-
loving lefty, first when his walk-off grand slam topped the Twins in 14 innings
on May 17, then more so when he finished the season with 41 home runs,
122 RBIs, and a .314 batting average. Nearly as productive in '03, Giambi was
diagnosed with a benign tumor in 2004 and missed half the season. Resurgent
in '05, he was Comeback Player of the Year, but eventually left New York after
2008.

Topps card pictured: 2003 #30. In 2003, Topps reprised its classic 1951 Red Backs and Blue Backs baseball
game cards, featuring Giambi on a Blue Back (#BB9).

JASON GIAMBI

1 B

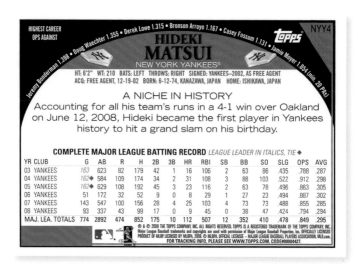

HIDEKI MATSUI

NEW YORK YANKEES®

HT: 6'2" WT: 210 BATS: LEFT THROWS: RIGHT SIGNED: YANKEES–2002, AS FREE AGENT
ACQ: FREE AGENT, 12-19-02 BORN: 6-12-74, KANAZAWA, JAPAN HOME: ISHIKAWA, JAPAN

A NICHE IN HISTORY

Accounting for all his team's runs in a 4-1 win over Oakland
on June 12, 2008, Hideki became the first player in Yankees
history to hit a grand slam on his birthday.

COMPLETE MAJOR LEAGUE BATTING RECORD *LEAGUE LEADER IN ITALICS, TIE ◆*

YR CLUB	G	AB	R	H	2B	3B	HR	RBI	SB	BB	SO	SLG	OPS	AVG
03 YANKEES	*163*	623	82	179	42	1	16	106	2	63	86	.435	.788	.287
04 YANKEES	*162◆*	584	109	174	34	2	31	108	3	88	103	.522	.912	.298
05 YANKEES	*162◆*	629	108	192	45	3	23	116	2	63	78	.496	.863	.305
06 YANKEES	51	172	32	52	9	0	8	29	1	27	23	.494	.887	.302
07 YANKEES	143	547	100	156	28	4	25	103	4	73	73	.488	.855	.285
08 YANKEES	93	337	43	99	17	0	9	45	0	38	47	.424	.794	.294
MAJ. LEA. TOTALS	774	2892	474	852	175	10	112	507	12	352	410	.478	.849	.295

HIDEKI MATSUI Matsui was a megastar back home, where the slugger known as Godzilla led the Yomiuri Giants to three Japan Series titles and won a trio of MVPs over 10 seasons. Expectations were high when he joined the Yankees for 2003, and Matsui hardly disappointed, hitting major league pitchers at a .287 clip, racking up 42 doubles, 16 homers, and 106 RBIs—and the first of two All-Star nods. He remained an everyday force in the Yankees lineup, particularly in postseason play. Godzilla terrified the Phillies in the 2009 World Series, going 8 for 13 with three home runs and eight RBIs to earn Series MVP honors.

Topps card pictured: 2009 #NYY4. This card illustrates Matsui's sweet and powerful swing, which in '09—Godzilla's first as a full-time DH—produced 28 home runs and 90 RBIs during the regular season.

World Series

YANKEES®
HIDEKI MATSUI

DH

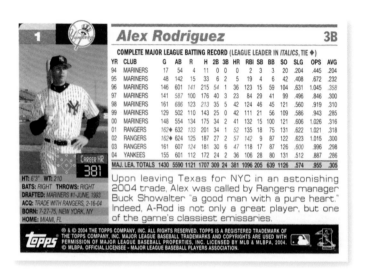

Alex Rodriguez 3B

COMPLETE MAJOR LEAGUE BATTING RECORD (LEAGUE LEADER IN *ITALICS*, TIE ◆)

YR	CLUB	G	AB	R	H	2B	3B	HR	RBI	SB	BB	SO	SLG	OPS	AVG
94	MARINERS	17	54	4	11	0	0	0	2	3	3	20	.204	.445	.204
95	MARINERS	48	142	15	33	6	2	5	19	4	6	42	.408	.672	.232
96	MARINERS	146	601	*141*	215	*54*	1	36	123	15	59	104	.631	1.045	.358
97	MARINERS	141	*587*	100	176	40	3	23	84	29	41	99	.496	.846	.300
98	MARINERS	161	*686*	123	*213*	35	5	42	124	46	45	121	.560	.919	.310
99	MARINERS	129	502	110	143	25	0	42	111	21	56	109	.586	.943	.285
00	MARINERS	148	554	134	175	34	2	41	132	15	100	121	.606	1.026	.316
01	RANGERS	*162*◆	632	*133*	201	34	1	*52*	135	18	75	131	.622	1.021	.318
02	RANGERS	*162*◆	624	125	187	27	2	*57*	*142*	9	87	122	.623	1.015	.300
03	RANGERS	161	607	*124*	181	30	6	*47*	118	17	87	126	.600	.996	.298
04	YANKEES	155	601	112	172	24	2	36	106	28	80	131	.512	.887	.286
MAJ. LEA. TOTALS		**1430**	**5590**	**1121**	**1707**	**309**	**24**	**381**	**1096**	**205**	**639**	**1126**	**.574**	**.955**	**.305**

CAREER HR
381

HT: *6'3"* WT: *210*
BATS: *RIGHT* THROWS: *RIGHT*
DRAFTED: *MARINERS #1-JUNE, 1993*
ACQ: *TRADE WITH RANGERS, 2-16-04*
BORN: *7-27-75, NEW YORK, NY*
HOME: *MIAMI, FL*

Upon leaving Texas for NYC in an astonishing 2004 trade, Alex was called by Rangers manager Buck Showalter "a good man with a pure heart." Indeed, A-Rod is not only a great player, but one of the game's classiest emissaries.

ALEX RODRIQUEZ The overall number-one draft pick in 1993 by the Mariners, A-Rod rammed through the minors and made his MLB debut at 18. In '94, his rookie season, he led the majors with a .358 batting average and 54 doubles and made his first of 14 All-Star teams. In 2003, two years after signing with Texas, he won his first MVP Award, and after joining the Yanks in 2004 was MVP again in '05 and '07. In 2009, Rodriguez exorcised his postseason demons, carrying the Yanks through the ALDS and ALCS on the way to their World Series win over Philadelphia—an unprecedented 27th title.

Topps card pictured: 2005 #1. Coming off his MVP season in 2004—A-Rod's first in pinstripes—Topps featured him not only on card #1 but also on Series 1 retail boxes and wrappers.

RODRIGUEZ

NEW YORK YANKEES®

ALEX RODRIGUEZ

2005

Yankees®

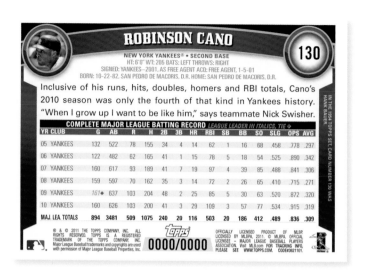

ROBINSON CANO 130

NEW YORK YANKEES® • SECOND BASE
HT: 6'0" WT: 205 BATS: LEFT THROWS: RIGHT
SIGNED: YANKEES—2001, AS FREE AGENT ACQ: FREE AGENT, 1-5-01
BORN: 10-22-82, SAN PEDRO DE MACORIS, D.R. HOME: SAN PEDRO DE MACORIS, D.R.

Inclusive of his runs, hits, doubles, homers and RBI totals, Cano's 2010 season was only the fourth of that kind in Yankees history. "When I grow up I want to be like him," says teammate Nick Swisher.

COMPLETE MAJOR LEAGUE BATTING RECORD *LEAGUE LEADER IN ITALICS, TIE ◆*

YR CLUB	G	AB	R	H	2B	3B	HR	RBI	SB	BB	SO	SLG	OPS	AVG
05 YANKEES	132	522	78	155	34	4	14	62	1	16	68	.458	.778	.297
06 YANKEES	122	482	62	165	41	1	15	78	5	18	54	.525	.890	.342
07 YANKEES	160	617	93	189	41	7	19	97	4	39	85	.488	.841	.306
08 YANKEES	159	597	70	162	35	3	14	72	2	26	65	.410	.715	.271
09 YANKEES	161◆	637	103	204	48	2	25	85	5	30	63	.520	.872	.320
10 YANKEES	160	626	103	200	41	3	29	109	3	57	77	.534	.915	.319
MAJ. LEA. TOTALS	894	3481	509	1075	240	20	116	503	20	186	412	.489	.836	.309

IN THE 1954 TOPPS SET CARD NUMBER 130 WAS HANK BAUER.

ROBINSON CANO   On May 27, 2005, in his first game against the Yankees' archrivals, the Boston Red Sox, Cano smashed his second major league homer, a two-run shot that tied a game the Yanks would win 6–3. "It was one of the best nights of my life," said Cano, whose dinger earned him his first Yankee Stadium curtain call. He finished '05 second in the Rookie of the Year balloting (after Huston Street) and next in line for Yankees greatness. Over the following five seasons, Cano averaged 184 hits, 41 doubles, 20 home runs, and 88 RBIs, hitting .311 with an .846 OPS.

Topps card pictured: 2011 #130. Cano is also included in Topps' 2011 Heritage Chrome set (#C147), a replica of the 1962 design. The retro card back refers to Robbie's .996 fielding percentage in 2010, a record for a Yankees second baseman.

ROBINSON CANO

SECOND BASE

NEW YORK YANKEES

NEW YORK YANKEES

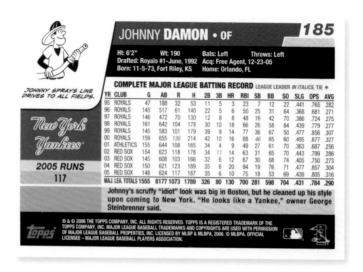

JOHNNY SPRAYS LINE
DRIVES TO ALL FIELDS.

New York
Yankees

2005 RUNS
117

JOHNNY **DAMON** • OF

185

Ht: 6'2"	Wt: 190	Bats: Left	Throws: Left
Drafted: Royals #1-June, 1992		Acq: Free Agent, 12-23-05	
Born: 11-5-73, Fort Riley, KS		Home: Orlando, FL	

COMPLETE MAJOR LEAGUE BATTING RECORD LEAGUE LEADER IN ITALICS, TIE ◆

YR	CLUB	G	AB	R	H	2B	3B	HR	RBI	SB	BB	SO	SLG	OPS	AVG
95	ROYALS	47	188	32	53	11	5	3	23	7	12	22	.441	.765	.282
96	ROYALS	145	517	61	140	22	5	6	50	25	31	64	.368	.681	.271
97	ROYALS	146	472	70	130	12	8	8	48	16	42	70	.386	.724	.275
98	ROYALS	161	642	104	178	30	10	18	66	26	58	84	.439	.779	.277
99	ROYALS	145	583	101	179	39	9	14	77	36	67	50	.477	.856	.307
00	ROYALS	159	655	136	214	42	10	16	88	46	65	60	.495	.877	.327
01	ATHLETICS	155	644	108	165	34	4	9	49	27	61	70	.363	.687	.256
02	RED SOX	154	623	118	178	34	11	14	63	31	65	70	.443	.799	.286
03	RED SOX	145	608	103	166	32	6	12	67	30	68	74	.405	.750	.273
04	RED SOX	150	621	123	189	35	6	20	94	19	76	71	.477	.857	.304
05	RED SOX	148	624	117	187	35	6	10	75	18	53	69	.439	.805	.316
MAJ. LEA. TOTALS		1555	6177	1073	1789	326	80	130	700	281	598	704	.431	.784	.290

Johnny's scruffy "idiot" look was big in Boston, but he cleaned up his style upon coming to New York. "He looks like a Yankee," owner George Steinbrenner said.

JOHNNY DAMON   Damon had a well-documented reputation when he signed with the Yankees in 2006 as a spirited player who got on base looking to wreak havoc with his speed and guile. Drafted by the Royals in '92, he developed his potent game in Kansas City before free agency landed him in Boston in 2001, where in '04 he helped the Red Sox win their first World Series since 1918. Two years later he was in the Bronx and still swinging a hot bat, averaging 159 hits, 31 doubles, and 19 home runs. He won another World Series in 2009, his final Yankees season, hitting .364 with a Damon-esque .440 OBP.

Topps card pictured: 2006 #185. The 2006 set goes way back in time, before baseball, to offer authentic "cut" signatures (cut from another source) of signers of the U.S. Constitution, including George Washington, Benjamin Franklin, James Madison, and Alexander Hamilton.

YANKEES®

JOHNNY DAMON

OUTFIELD

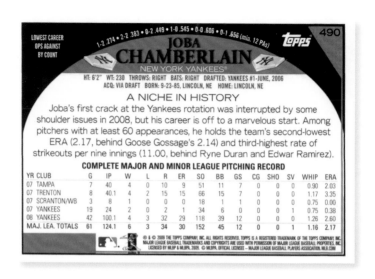

JOBA CHAMBERLAIN   Yankees fans weren't sure what to expect when this huge kid from Nebraska took the mound for the first time in August 2007. The team, however, knew that Joba—a childhood nickname that stuck—could strike out hitters with an upper-90s fastball. He fanned his first batter, then dozens more, often with fist-pumping flair, and the Yanks had a new bullpen weapon for the '07 postseason. A freakish swarm of insects in Cleveland undid Joba, and the Yankees, and he's since been a starter and reliever. Surgery ended his 2011 season, but the bullpen is where Joba's fate—and blazing fastball—seems destined.

Topps card pictured: 2009 #490A. Topps proved itself prescient in its choice of two players to picture on the 2009 retail packs, Ryan Howard and Alex Rodriguez, who would square off in that year's World Series, with A-Rod and the Yanks prevailing in six games.

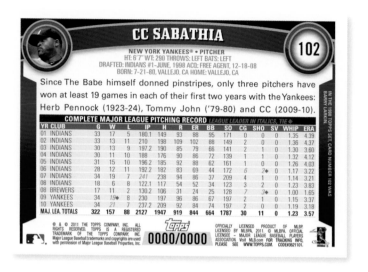

CC SABATHIA   When Sabathia signed a seven-year deal to join the Yankees in 2009, the team had little doubt that the big man would become their ace. The 6-foot-7, 290-pound lefty had won the 2007 AL Cy Young with Cleveland, and after the Indians traded him midseason '08 to Milwaukee, he went 11–2 in leading the Brewers to the postseason. In his first campaign in pinstripes, CC tied three others for most MLB wins (19) and paced the Yanks to their 27th world championship. With a win in the Division Series versus Minnesota and a two-win, MVP performance in the Championship Series versus Los Angeles, he gave up three earned runs in 22.2 innings pitched.

Topps card pictured: 2011 #102. The 2011 set celebrates the company's 60th anniversary of producing baseball cards sets. The 155 Diamond Die-Cut cards feature current and legendary stars.

CC SABATHIA

PITCHER

NEW YORK YANKEES

NEW YORK YANKEES

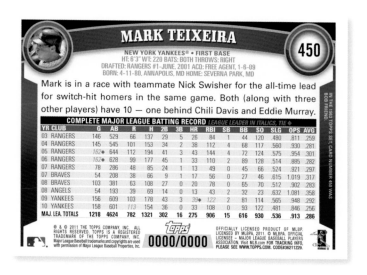

MARK TEIXEIRA

NEW YORK YANKEES® • FIRST BASE
HT: 6'3" WT: 220 BATS: BOTH THROWS: RIGHT
DRAFTED: RANGERS #1–JUNE, 2001 ACQ: FREE AGENT, 1-6-09
BORN: 4-11-80, ANNAPOLIS, MD HOME: SEVERNA PARK, MD

450

Mark is in a race with teammate Nick Swisher for the all-time lead for switch-hit homers in the same game. Both (along with three other players) have 10 — one behind Chili Davis and Eddie Murray.

COMPLETE MAJOR LEAGUE BATTING RECORD *LEAGUE LEADER IN ITALICS, TIE ◆*

YR CLUB	G	AB	R	H	2B	3B	HR	RBI	SB	BB	SO	SLG	OPS	AVG
03 RANGERS	146	529	66	137	29	5	26	84	1	44	120	.480	.811	.259
04 RANGERS	145	545	101	153	34	2	38	112	4	68	117	.560	.930	.281
05 RANGERS	*162◆*	644	112	194	41	3	43	144	4	72	124	.575	.954	.301
06 RANGERS	*162◆*	628	99	177	45	1	33	110	2	89	128	.514	.885	.282
07 RANGERS	78	286	48	85	24	1	13	49	0	45	66	.524	.921	.297
07 BRAVES	54	208	38	66	9	1	17	56	0	27	46	.615	1.019	.317
08 BRAVES	103	381	63	108	27	0	20	78	0	65	70	.512	.902	.283
08 ANGELS	54	193	39	69	14	0	13	43	2	32	23	.632	1.081	.358
09 YANKEES	156	609	103	178	43	3	*39◆*	*122*	2	81	114	.565	.948	.292
10 YANKEES	158	601	*113*	154	36	0	33	108	0	93	122	.481	.846	.256
MAJ. LEA. TOTALS	**1218**	**4624**	**782**	**1321**	**302**	**16**	**275**	**906**	**15**	**616**	**930**	**.536**	**.913**	**.286**

IN THE 1983 TOPPS SET, CARD NUMBER 450 WAS BOB FRIEND.

MARK TEIXEIRA Teixeira was a perfect fit in the new Yankee Stadium, arriving for its debut season and quickly establishing himself as the Yankees latest power-hitting, slick-fielding first baseman. He had set the bar high for himself over four-plus seasons with Texas, most notably in 2005, when he hit .301 with 43 hits, 41 doubles, 144 RBIs, and a whopping .954 OPS. In his first year as a Yankee, Tex was an All-Star and a runner-up in the MVP vote. He finished at .292, led the AL in homers (39) and RBIs (122), won his third Gold Glove, and wrapped things up with a World Series ring.

Topps card pictured: 2011 #450A. The switch-hitting home run record referred to on this card's back was set by Teixeira on August 3, 2011, when he hit homers at U.S. Cellular Field in Chicago from both sides of the plate, passing Eddie Murray and Chili Davis, who each did it 11 times.

MARK TEIXEIRA

FIRST BASE

NEW YORK YANKEES
NEW YORK YANKEES

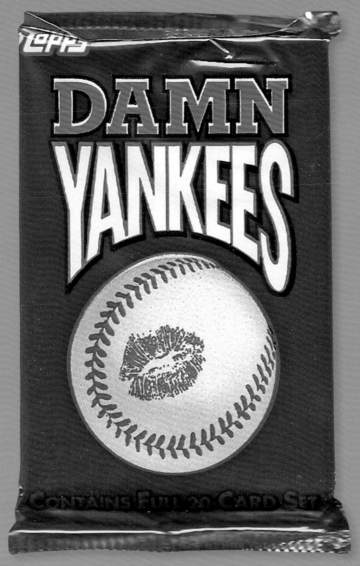

Foil pack for the 1994 special 20-card Topps set connected with the Broadway revival of *Damn Yankees*

PART 7 · GREAT MOMENTS, RISING STARS & MANAGERS

The Yankees, to date, have won 27 world championships, and the players on the team's long list of greats have been the nucleus of each and every one. There is another group of Yankees, however, who also deserve a lot of credit. Although they might not have been with the club for years, or weren't everyday players, they've made memorable, game-changing contributions—pitching a no-hitter, coming up with a clutch hit, providing game-saving relief out of the bullpen, smashing a walk-off homer. These instant heroes step up at just the right time, and proudly take their well-deserved places in Yankees history.

While there will never be another Babe Ruth, Mickey Mantle, or Mariano Rivera, that doesn't prevent fans from sizing up young players working their way through the Yankees farm system, or from salivating over another team's pitching ace as he approaches free agency. And, of course, once they join the Yanks and start producing, the value of their Topps baseball cards goes up accordingly. That's why we've identified a handful of current players whose stock is rising along with the Yankees' greatness.

When baseball teams are winning, we applaud the players. When they lose, we blame the manager. Yankees fans have had a lot of great players to cheer for along the way to 27 championships, so the skippers of those teams deserve a ton of praise. That keeps the expectations sky high—it's the World Series or bust every season—and with the 24/7 scrutiny of New York's intense media scene, Yankees managers certainly earn their pinstripes. With all that in mind, we honor the honchos who've been heads above others in leading the Yanks to more victories than any other team in baseball history.

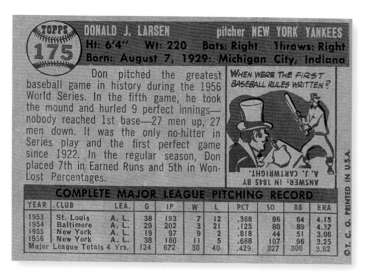

LARSENY: YANKS ROB DODGERS OF HITS Since 1900, only 18 pitchers have thrown a perfect game, meaning that no batter reaches base—27 up, 27 down. But when Larsen threw a perfect Game 5 in the 1956 World Series against the Brooklyn Dodgers, baseball saw a feat that hadn't been glimpsed before or since. The big righty had gone 11–5 with a 3.26 ERA in his second year with the Yankees, but was shelled in Game 2's loss. In Game 5, though, "his stuff was good, good, good," said catcher Yogi Berra, who, after pinch hitter Dale Mitchell took a called third strike to end the game, famously—perfectly—jumped into Larsen's arms.

Topps card pictured: 1957 #175. Series 1 of the 1957 set is stacked with superstars, featuring 7 Hall of Famers in the first 20 cards and 23 in the first 100 cards.

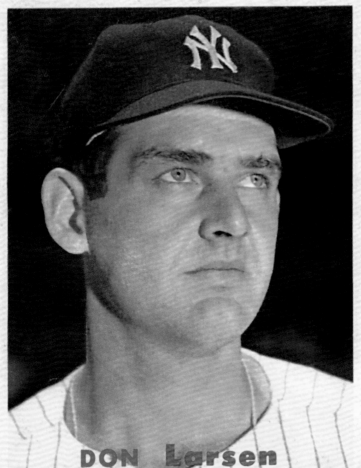

DON **Larsen**

NEW YORK YANKEES PITCHER

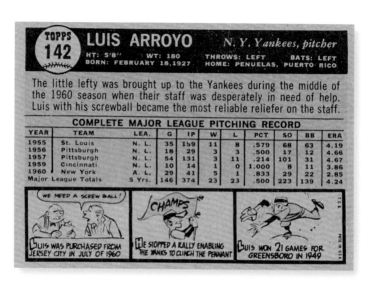

COMPLETE MAJOR LEAGUE PITCHING RECORD

YEAR	TEAM	LEA.	G	IP	W	L	PCT	SO	BB	ERA
1955	St. Louis	N. L.	35	159	11	8	.579	68	63	4.19
1956	Pittsburgh	N. L.	18	29	3	3	.500	17	12	4.66
1957	Pittsburgh	N. L.	54	131	3	11	.214	101	31	4.67
1959	Cincinnati	N. L.	10	14	1	0	1.000	8	11	3.86
1960	New York	A. L.	29	41	5	1	.833	29	22	2.85
Major League Totals		5 Yrs.	146	374	23	23	.500	223	139	4.24

OH, BOY-O, ARROYO! Roger Maris smashed his historic 61st home run on the 1961 season's final day, sending the Yankees into the World Series versus the Cardinals on a high note. Meanwhile, Arroyo's screwball had made him the Yanks' bullpen ace, leading to a 15–5 record and an AL-best 29 saves. His greatest moment, however, came in Game 3 of the '61 Series at Crosley Field. With the score tied 2–2, Arroyo pitched a scoreless eighth inning. Maris, appropriately, hit a homer in the top of the ninth, Arroyo blanked the Cards in their half, and the Yanks went on to win the Series in five games.

Topps card pictured: 1961 #142. The 1961 set marked the debut of separate, numbered checklist cards.

LUIS ARROYO
Pitcher

New York
Yankees

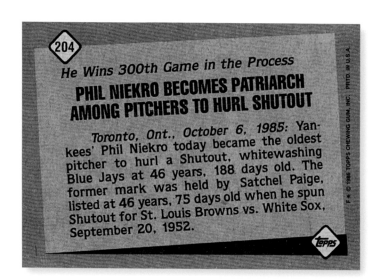

KNUCKSIE NOTCHES NUMBER 300 Niekro brought his confounding knuckleball to the Bronx in 1984. Although 45 years old, and already with 254 wins under his belt, Knucksie still had plenty of life in his right arm—and proved it on October 6, 1985, at Yankee Stadium. Having failed in four previous starts, he defeated the Blue Jays, 8–0, and finally won his 300th game, becoming the 18th member of that exclusive pitchers' club. In the process, Niekro also became the oldest pitcher (46 years, 188 days) to record a shutout. Incredibly, he didn't throw his signature knuckleball until the very last hitter, striking out Jeff Burroughs with three nasty knucklers.

Topps card pictured: 1986 #204. The 1986 set includes a special Pete Rose subset (#2–#7), made up of reproductions of the all-time-hits leader's Topps cards from 1963 to 1985, four to a card.

'85 RECORD BREAKER

PHIL NIEKRO, NEW YORK YANKEES
Oldest Pitcher to Hurl Shutout

350   **JIM ABBOTT**

HT: 6'3"   WT: 210   THROWS: LEFT   BATS: LEFT
DRFT: ANGELS #1-JUNE, 1988   ACQ: TRADE, 12-6-92
BORN: 9-19-67 , FLINT, MI
HOME: NEWPORT BEACH, CA

COMPLETE MAJOR LEAGUE PITCHING RECORD

YR	CLUB	G	IP	W	L	R	ER	SO	BB	GS	CG	SHO	SV	ERA
89	ANGELS	29	181.1	12	12	95	79	115	74	29	4		2	0	3.92
90	ANGELS	33	211.2	10	14	116	106	105	72	33	4		1	0	4.51
91	ANGELS	34	243	18	11	85	78	158	73	34	5		1	0	2.89
92	ANGELS	29	211	7	15	73	65	130	68	29	7		0	0	2.77
93	YANKEES	32	214	11	14	115	104	95	73	32	4		1	0	4.37
MAJ. LEA. TOTALS		157	1061	58	66	484	432	603	360	157	24		5	0	3.66

On 9-4-93, Jim stymied the Indians with the first Yankee no-hitter in 10 years. He has not allowed a HR to a LH batter since 9-19-91, spanning 443 innings.

YES! ABBOTT THROWS A NO-NO! Undaunted courage met pinstripe pride when Jim Abbott made baseball history at Yankee Stadium on September 4, 1993. Abbott was born without a right hand but persevered with his left to become a superb ballplayer in high school, college, and international competition, ultimately winning a gold medal at the 1988 Summer Olympics. He was the Angels' number-one draft pick that year and jumped right to the majors. After four seasons filled with flashes of brilliance, Abbott was traded to the Yankees, where he enjoyed his magical moment—throwing a 4–0 no-hitter against the Cleveland Indians.

Topps card pictured: 1994 #350. Abbott's rookie card (#1T), from the Topps 1988 Traded subset, pictures him from the U.S. Olympic baseball team that won the gold medal. Abbott was the starter in the decisive game.

Jim Abbott

YANKEES
P

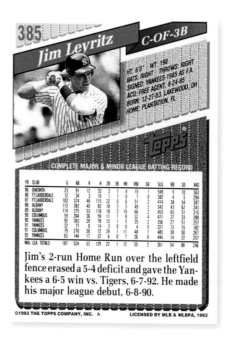

385

Jim Leyritz

C-OF-3B

HT: 6'0" WT: 190
BATS: RIGHT THROWS: RIGHT
SIGNED: YANKEES-1985 AS F.A.
ACQ: FREE AGENT, 8-24-85
BORN: 12-27-63, LAKEWOOD, OH
HOME: PLANTATION, FL

COMPLETE MAJOR & MINOR LEAGUE BATTING RECORD

YR	CLUB	G	AB	R	H	2B	3B	HR	RBI	SB	SLG	BB	SO	AVG
85	ONEONTA	23	91	12	33	3	1	4	15	1	549	5	10	363
86	FT.LAUDERDALE	12	34	3	10	1	1	0	1	0	382	4	5	294
87	FT.LAUDERDALE	102	374	48	115	22	0	6	51	2	414	38	54	307
88	ALBANY	112	382	40	92	18	3	5	49	3	343	43	62	241
89	ALBANY	114	375	53	118	18	2	10	66	2	453	65	51	315
90	COLUMBUS	59	204	36	59	11	1	8	32	4	471	37	33	289
90	YANKEES	92	303	28	78	13	1	5	25	2	356	27	51	257
91	YANKEES	32	77	8	14	3	0	0	4	0	221	13	15	182
91	COLUMBUS	79	270	50	72	24	1	11	48	1	485	38	50	267
92	YANKEES	63	144	17	37	6	0	7	26	0	444	14	22	257
	MAJ. LEA. TOTALS	187	524	53	129	22	1	12	55	2	361	54	88	246

Jim's 2-run Home Run over the leftfield fence erased a 5-4 deficit and gave the Yankees a 6-5 win vs. Tigers, 6-7-92. He made his major league debut, 6-8-90.

©1993 THE TOPPS COMPANY, INC. A   LICENSED BY MLB & MLBPA, 1993

LEYRITZ HOMER BURNS ATLANTA Leyritz will always be remembered for the dramatic, game-tying home run he lofted into the left-field seats at Atlanta-Fulton County Stadium in the pivotal Game 4 of the 1996 World Series. The Braves had demolished the Yanks in the first two games in New York, dropped Game 3 at home, and were leading 6–0 after five innings of Game 4. His Braves still up by three runs in the eighth, closer Mark Wohlers delivered a hanging slider that left the yard—and emblazoned Leyritz's name in Yankees history after the Bombers went on to win that battle, and the next two, to capture the Series.

Topps card pictured: 1993 #385. In 1993, Topps marked the debut seasons of MLB's newest expansion teams, the Colorado Rockies and Florida Marlins, with special factory sets.

JIM LEYRITZ

YANKEES

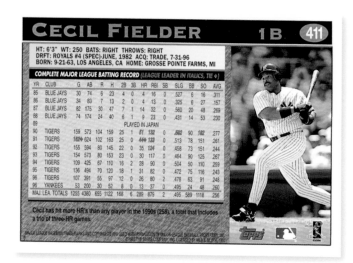

CECIL FIELDER 1B 411

HT: 6'3" WT: 250 BATS: RIGHT THROWS: RIGHT
DRFT: ROYALS #4 (SPEC)-JUNE, 1982 ACQ: TRADE, 7-31-96
BORN: 9-21-63, LOS ANGELES, CA HOME: GROSSE POINTE FARMS, MI

COMPLETE MAJOR LEAGUE BATTING RECORD (LEAGUE LEADER IN ITALICS, TIE ◊)

YR	CLUB	G	AB	R	H	2B	3B	HR	RBI	SB	SLG	BB	SO	AVG
85	BLUE JAYS	30	74	6	23	4	0	4	16	0	.527	6	16	.311
86	BLUE JAYS	34	83	7	13	2	0	4	13	0	.325	6	27	.157
87	BLUE JAYS	82	175	30	47	7	1	14	32	0	.560	20	48	.269
88	BLUE JAYS	74	174	24	40	6	1	9	23	0	.431	14	53	.230
89						PLAYED IN JAPAN								
90	TIGERS	159	573	104	159	25	1	51	132	0	.592	90	182	.277
91	TIGERS	162	624	102	163	25	0	44	133	0	.513	78	151	.261
92	TIGERS	155	594	80	145	22	0	35	124	0	.458	73	151	.244
93	TIGERS	154	573	80	153	23	0	30	117	0	.464	90	125	.267
94	TIGERS	109	425	67	110	16	2	28	90	0	.504	50	110	.259
95	TIGERS	136	494	70	120	18	1	31	82	0	.472	75	116	.243
96	TIGERS	107	391	55	97	12	0	26	80	2	.478	63	91	.248
96	YANKEES	53	200	30	52	8	0	13	37	0	.495	24	48	.260
MAJ. LEA. TOTALS		1255	4380	655	1122	168	6	289	879	2	.495	589	1118	.256

Cecil has hit more HR's than any player in the 1990s (258), a total that includes a trio of three-HR games.

MAJOR LEAGUE BASEBALL TRADEMARKS AND COPYRIGHTS ARE USED WITH PERMISSION OF MAJOR LEAGUE BASEBALL PROPERTIES, INC. ©1997 THE TOPPS COMPANY, INC. LICENSED BY MLB & MLBPA 1997

WHO'S YOUR BIG DADDY? Fielder wasn't a prototypical power hitter in his four seasons as a part-timer with the Blue Jays, but after a season in Japan, he signed with Detroit in 1990 and smashed a league-high 51 homers. His bulging stats had dwindled by the time a July 1996 trade brought him to the Yankees, but he still put a jolt in the team's offense, especially in postseason play. Big Daddy blasted three homers and drove in 12 runs in the first two rounds, then his RBI double in Game 5 of the World Series versus Atlanta scored the game's only run and helped propel the Yanks to the title.

Topps card pictured: 1997 #411. In 1996, fans so enjoyed reprints of past Mickey Mantle cards—issued by Topps and Bowman—that Topps included another 16 in the '97 set.

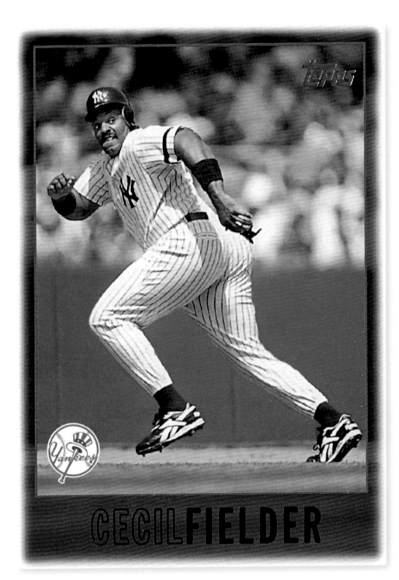

CECILFIELDER

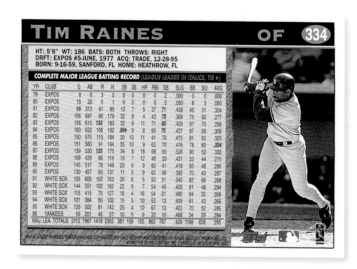

TIM RAINES — OF — 334

HT: 5'8" WT: 186 BATS: BOTH THROWS: RIGHT
DRFT: EXPOS #5-JUNE, 1977 ACQ: TRADE, 12-28-95
BORN: 9-16-59, SANFORD, FL HOME: HEATHROW, FL

COMPLETE MAJOR LEAGUE BATTING RECORD *(LEAGUE LEADER IN ITALICS, TIE ◆)*

YR	CLUB	G	AB	R	H	2B	3B	HR	RBI	SB	SLG	BB	SO	AVG
79	EXPOS	6	0	3	0	0	0	0	0	2	.000	0	0	.000
80	EXPOS	15	20	5	1	0	0	0	0	5	.050	6	3	.050
81	EXPOS	88	313	61	95	13	7	5	37	*71*	.438	45	31	.304
82	EXPOS	156	647	90	179	32	8	4	43	*78*	.369	75	83	.277
83	EXPOS	156	615	*133*	183	32	8	11	71	*90*	.429	97	70	.298
84	EXPOS	160	622	106	192	*38◆*	9	8	60	*75*	.437	87	69	.309
85	EXPOS	150	575	115	184	30	13	11	41	70	.475	81	60	.320
86	EXPOS	151	580	91	194	35	10	9	62	70	.476	78	60	*.334*
87	EXPOS	139	530	*123*	175	34	8	18	68	50	.526	90	52	.330
88	EXPOS	109	429	66	116	19	7	12	48	33	.431	53	44	.270
89	EXPOS	145	517	76	148	29	6	9	60	41	.418	93	48	.286
90	EXPOS	130	457	65	131	11	5	9	62	49	.392	70	43	.287
91	WHITE SOX	155	609	102	163	20	6	5	50	51	.345	83	68	.268
92	WHITE SOX	144	551	102	162	22	9	7	54	45	.405	81	48	.294
93	WHITE SOX	115	415	75	127	16	4	16	54	21	.480	64	35	.306
94	WHITE SOX	101	384	80	102	15	5	10	52	13	.409	61	43	.266
95	WHITE SOX	133	502	81	143	25	4	12	67	13	.522	70	52	.285
96	YANKEES	59	201	45	57	10	0	9	33	10	.468	34	29	.284
	MAJ. LEA. TOTALS	2112	7967	1419	2352	381	109	155	862	787	.429	1168	838	.295

RAINES POURS IT ON   The Yankees continued their knack of bringing in superstars perhaps past their prime but still with plenty left in their tanks when they added Raines to the roster in 1996. A seven-time All-Star with the Expos during the '80s, he'd led the NL in steals four straight years and averaged over .300. Even at age 36 and playing part-time as a designated hitter or in left field, Raines gave the Yanks another offensive weapon, plus veteran leadership in the clubhouse, especially during the 1996 playoffs. He contributed 11 hits en route to earning his first, well-deserved World Series ring.

Topps card pictured: 1997 #334. Raines's 1981 rookie card (#479) pictures him with two other Expos rookies. Coincidentally, 19 years later, his son Tim Raines Jr. was pictured on a Topps Prospects card (2000 #445) with two other up-and-comers.

TIMRAINES

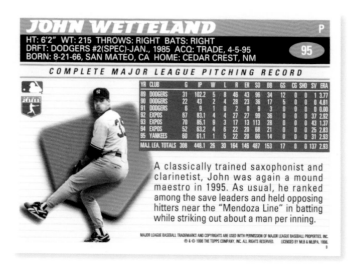

JOHN WETTELAND P

HT: 6'2" WT: 215 THROWS: RIGHT BATS: RIGHT
DRFT: DODGERS #2(SPEC)-JAN., 1985 ACQ: TRADE, 4-5-95
BORN: 8-21-66, SAN MATEO, CA HOME: CEDAR CREST, NM

95

COMPLETE MAJOR LEAGUE PITCHING RECORD

YR	CLUB	G	IP	W	L	R	ER	SO	BB	GS	CG	SHO	SV	ERA
89	DODGERS	31	102.2	5	8	46	43	96	34	12	0	1	3.77	
90	DODGERS	22	43	2	4	28	23	36	17	5	0	0	4.81	
91	DODGERS	6	9	1	0	2	0	9	3	0	0	0	0.00	
92	EXPOS	67	83.1	4	4	27	27	99	36	0	0	37	2.92	
93	EXPOS	70	85.1	9	3	17	13	113	28	0	0	43	1.37	
94	EXPOS	52	63.2	4	6	22	20	68	21	0	0	25	2.83	
95	YANKEES	60	61.1	1	5	22	20	66	14	0	0	31	2.93	
MAJ. LEA. TOTALS		308	448.1	26	30	164	146	487	153	17	0	137	2.93	

A classically trained saxophonist and
clarinetist, John was again a mound
maestro in 1995. As usual, he ranked
among the save leaders and held opposing
hitters near the "Mendoza Line" in batting
while striking out about a man per inning.

WETTELAND MOPS UP '96 PLAYOFFS   Wetteland was arguably the most dominant closer of the 1990s, starting out with the Dodgers before moving to the Expos, the Reds, and then, in 1995, the Yankees. He led the American League with 43 saves in '96 as the Yanks returned to the World Series for the first time since 1981. After saving two games in the ALDS versus Texas and another in the ALCS versus Baltimore, Wetteland was nearly flawless in the Fall Classic versus Atlanta. Giving up only four hits, one walk, and one earned run over five games and 4.1 innings pitched, he saved all four Yankees victories and earned Series MVP honors.

Topps card pictured: 1996 #95. The Topps 1996 set featured Kirby Puckett and Tony Gwynn not only on card packs but also as analysts of players in a special 40-card subset, featuring 20 stars from each league. Yankees Don Mattingly and Paul O'Neill were included.

JOHN WETTELAND

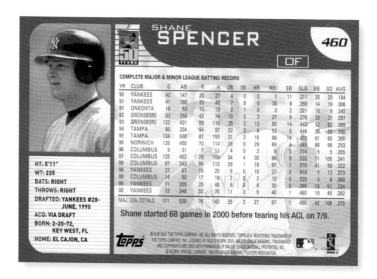

SHANE **SPENCER**

460

OF

COMPLETE MAJOR & MINOR LEAGUE BATTING RECORD

YR	CLUB	G	AB	R	H	2B	3B	HR	RBI	SB	SLG	BB	SO	AVG
90	YANKEES	42	147	20	27	4	0	0	7	11	.211	20	23	.184
91	YANKEES	41	160	25	49	7	0	0	30	8	.350	14	19	.306
91	ONEONTA	18	53	10	13	2	1	0	3	2	.321	10	9	.245
92	GREENSBORO	83	258	43	74	10	2	3	27	8	.376	33	37	.287
93	GREENSBORO	122	431	89	116	35	2	12	80	14	.443	52	62	.269
94	TAMPA	90	334	44	97	22	3	8	53	5	.446	30	53	.290
95	TAMPA	134	500	87	150	31	3	16	88	14	.470	61	60	.300
96	NORWICH	126	450	70	114	16	0	29	89	4	.489	68	99	.253
96	COLUMBUS	9	31	7	11	4	0	3	6	0	.774	5	5	.355
97	COLUMBUS	125	452	78	109	34	4	30	86	0	.533	71	105	.241
98	COLUMBUS	87	342	66	110	29	1	18	67	1	.570	41	59	.322
98	YANKEES	27	67	18	25	6	0	10	27	0	.910	5	12	.373
99	COLUMBUS	14	50	17	18	2	0	2	10	0	.520	9	8	.360
99	YANKEES	71	205	25	48	8	0	8	20	0	.390	18	51	.234
00	YANKEES	73	248	33	70	11	3	9	40	1	.460	19	45	.282
MAJ. LEA. TOTALS		171	520	76	143	25	3	27	87	1	.490	42	108	.275

HT: 5'11"
WT: 225
BATS: RIGHT
THROWS: RIGHT
DRAFTED: YANKEES #28-
JUNE, 1990
ACQ: VIA DRAFT
BORN: 2-20-72,
KEY WEST, FL
HOME: EL CAJON, CA

Shane started 68 games in 2000 before tearing his ACL on 7/9.

SHANE GOES DEEP . . . AGAIN . . . AND AGAIN . . . Seemingly out of nowhere, like the title character in the touching 1953 western *Shane*, the Yankees' Shane rode heroically into the Bronx and touched 'em all, repeatedly. It was September 1998 and the Bombers were well on their way to winning a record 114 regular-season games and first of three consecutive world championships. Shane would be an unexpected exclamation point, smashing 10 home runs—including three grand slams—in just 67 at-bats, instantly endearing himself to the fans. The cheering continued in the postseason, when he blasted a pair of dingers in the Division Series and finished the playoffs with a lusty .632 slugging percentage.

Topps card pictured: 2001 #460. Spencer enjoyed his Topps debut in 1996. The burgeoning Bomber was featured on a Prospects card (#436) along with Roger Cedeno, Derrick Gibson, and Ben Grieve.

Shane **SPENCER**

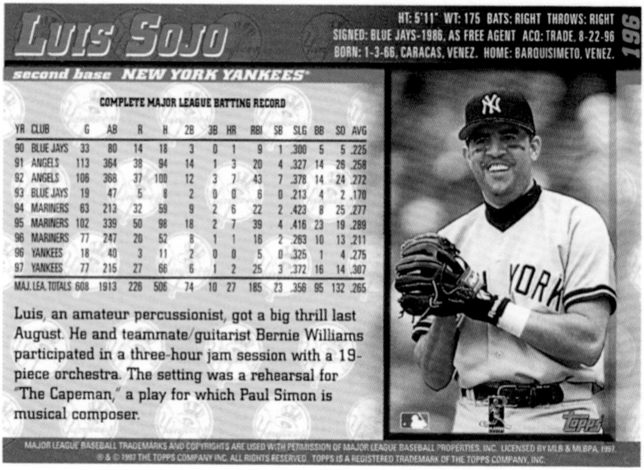
Luis Sojo
HT: 5'11" WT: 175 BATS: RIGHT THROWS: RIGHT
SIGNED: BLUE JAYS-1986, AS FREE AGENT ACQ: TRADE, 8-22-96
BORN: 1-3-66, CARACAS, VENEZ. HOME: BARQUISIMETO, VENEZ.
196
second base NEW YORK YANKEES
COMPLETE MAJOR LEAGUE BATTING RECORD
YR CLUB G AB R H 2B 3B HR RBI SB SLG BB SO AVG
90 BLUE JAYS 33 80 14 18 3 0 1 9 1 .300 5 5 .225
91 ANGELS 113 364 38 94 14 1 3 20 4 .327 14 26 .258
92 ANGELS 106 368 37 100 12 3 7 43 7 .378 14 24 .272
93 BLUE JAYS 19 47 5 8 2 0 0 6 0 .213 4 2 .170
94 MARINERS 63 213 32 59 9 2 6 22 2 .423 8 25 .277
95 MARINERS 102 339 50 98 18 2 7 39 4 .416 23 19 .289
96 MARINERS 77 247 20 52 8 1 1 16 2 .263 10 13 .211
96 YANKEES 18 40 3 11 2 0 0 5 0 .325 1 4 .275
97 YANKEES 77 215 27 66 6 1 2 25 3 .372 16 14 .307
MAJ. LEA. TOTALS 608 1913 226 506 74 10 27 185 23 .356 95 132 .265
Luis, an amateur percussionist, got a big thrill last August. He and teammate/guitarist Bernie Williams participated in a three-hour jam session with a 19-piece orchestra. The setting was a rehearsal for "The Capeman," a play for which Paul Simon is musical composer.
Topps
MAJOR LEAGUE BASEBALL TRADEMARKS AND COPYRIGHTS ARE USED WITH PERMISSION OF MAJOR LEAGUE BASEBALL PROPERTIES, INC. LICENSED BY MLB & MLBPA 1997.
® & © 1997 THE TOPPS COMPANY INC. ALL RIGHTS RESERVED. TOPPS IS A REGISTERED TRADEMARK OF THE TOPPS COMPANY, INC.

METS TO YANKS: SAY IT AIN'T SOJO When the Yankees' Luis Sojo came to bat in the bottom of the eighth inning in Game 5 of the 2000 Subway Series, his role as the ultimate utility man was about to be realized. Sojo had been on New York's three World Championship teams since 1996, playing all over the infield and delivering one clutch hit after another. Regardless, Mets starter Al Leiter, tiring after 8.2 innings, was still on the mound with the score tied 2–2 and his team facing elimination. Sojo slapped a two-RBI single, sending the Yanks to their third straight title and Sojo on to World Series hero status.

Topps card pictured: 1998 #196. Sojo retired after the 2003 season, then became the Yankees' third base coach for two seasons. He managed the Class A Tampa Yankees from 2006 to 2009. In 2011, he returned to the helm in Tampa.

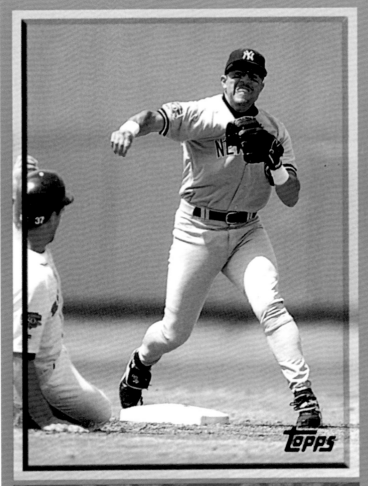

LUIS SOJO

NEW YORK YANKEES

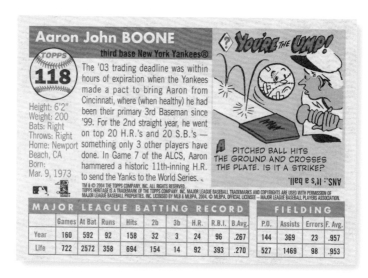

Aaron John BOONE

third base New York Yankees®

TOPPS

118

Height: 6'2"
Weight: 200
Bats: Right
Throws: Right
Home: Newport Beach, CA
Born: Mar. 9, 1973

The '03 trading deadline was within hours of expiration when the Yankees made a pact to bring Aaron from Cincinnati, where (when healthy) he had been their primary 3rd Baseman since '99. For the 2nd straight year, he went on top 20 H.R.'s and 20 S.B.'s — something only 3 other players have done. In Game 7 of the ALCS, Aaron hammered a historic 11th-inning H.R. to send the Yanks to the World Series.

YOU'RE THE UMP!

PITCHED BALL HITS THE GROUND AND CROSSES THE PLATE. IS IT A STRIKE?

ANS: It's a ball.

TM & © 2004 THE TOPPS COMPANY, INC. ALL RIGHTS RESERVED.
TOPPS HERITAGE IS A TRADEMARK OF THE TOPPS COMPANY, INC. MAJOR LEAGUE BASEBALL TRADEMARKS AND COPYRIGHTS ARE USED WITH PERMISSION OF MAJOR LEAGUE BASEBALL PROPERTIES, INC. LICENSED BY MLB & MLBPA, 2004. © MLBPA. OFFICIAL LICENSEE – MAJOR LEAGUE BASEBALL PLAYERS ASSOCIATION.

MAJOR LEAGUE BATTING RECORD										FIELDING			
	Games	At Bat	Runs	Hits	2b	3b	H.R.	R.B.I.	B.Avg.	P.O.	Assists	Errors	F. Avg.
Year	160	592	92	158	32	3	24	96	.267	144	369	23	.957
Life	722	2572	358	694	154	14	92	393	.270	527	1469	98	.953

BOONE'S BLAST BURIES BOSOX   No Yankees hero may be more unlikely than Aaron Boone was in the 2003 American League Championship Series against the dreaded Red Sox. He had enjoyed an All-Star first half of the season with the Reds, then was traded to the Yankees to shore up Joe Torre's bench. In the decisive Game 7 in the Bronx, the Yanks rallied from a 5–2 deficit against Pedro Martinez and went into extra innings. In the bottom of the 11th, up against knuckleballer Tim Wakefield, Boone launched a walk-off homer that sailed into the left-field stands—and lofted "the Boonebino" into Yankees immortality.

Topps card pictured: 2004 Topps Heritage #118. This is a replica of Topps' 1955 cards, which happened to feature Boone's grandfather, Ray Boone, then a slugging third baseman for the Tigers.

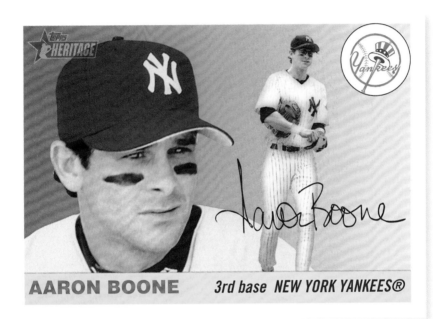

AARON BOONE   *3rd base*   **NEW YORK YANKEES®**

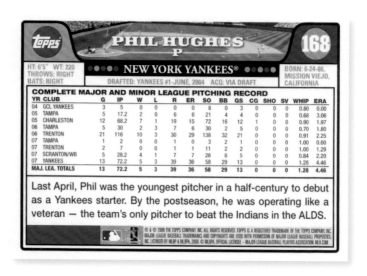

Topps **PHIL HUGHES** **168**
P

HT: 6'5" WT: 220
THROWS: RIGHT
BATS: RIGHT

●●●● **NEW YORK YANKEES®** ●●●●
DRAFTED: YANKEES #1-JUNE, 2004 ACQ: VIA DRAFT

BORN: 6-24-86,
MISSION VIEJO,
CALIFORNIA

COMPLETE MAJOR AND MINOR LEAGUE PITCHING RECORD

YR	CLUB	G	IP	W	L	R	ER	SO	BB	GS	CG	SHO	SV	WHIP	ERA
04	GCL YANKEES	3	5	0	0	0	0	8	0	3	0	0	0	0.80	0.00
05	TAMPA	5	17.2	2	0	6	6	21	4	4	0	0	0	0.68	3.06
05	CHARLESTON	12	68.2	7	1	19	15	72	16	12	1	0	0	0.90	1.97
06	TAMPA	5	30	2	3	7	6	30	2	5	0	0	0	0.70	1.80
06	TRENTON	21	116	10	3	30	29	138	32	21	0	0	0	0.91	2.25
07	TAMPA	1	2	0	0	1	0	3	2	1	0	0	0	1.00	0.00
07	TRENTON	2	7	0	0	1	1	11	2	2	0	0	0	1.00	1.29
07	SCRANTON/WB	5	28.2	4	1	7	7	28	8	5	0	0	0	0.84	2.20
07	YANKEES	13	72.2	5	3	39	36	58	29	13	0	0	0	1.28	4.46
MAJ. LEA. TOTALS		13	72.2	5	3	39	36	58	29	13	0	0	0	1.28	4.46

Last April, Phil was the youngest pitcher in a half-century to debut as a Yankees starter. By the postseason, he was operating like a veteran — the team's only pitcher to beat the Indians in the ALDS.

PHIL HUGHES Hughes was only 21 when he debuted as the Yankees' top pitching prospect on April 26, 2007. Although he surrendered four earned runs over 4.1 innings pitched in a 6–0 loss to Toronto, his mid-90s fastball and beyond-his-years demeanor kept him in the majors. In his second start, Hughes was pitching a no-hitter in Texas before a pulled hamstring sidelined him until August. In 2009, Hughes moved to the bullpen and became a dominant setup man as the Yankees rolled to their 27th world championship. Back in the rotation in 2010, he went 18–8, made the All-Star team, and maintained his potential greatness, though injuries slowed him in 2011.

Topps card pictured: 2008 #168. Hughes's rookie card (#T78) was issued in 2004, identifying the California-born righty not only as a promising Yankees draft pick but also as a Red Sox fan while growing up.

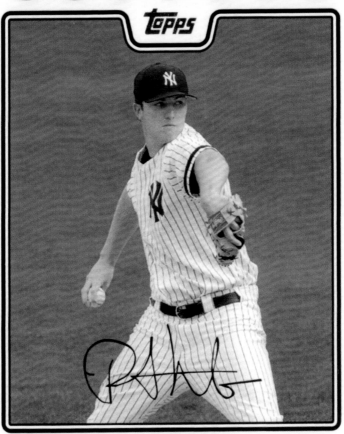

PHIL HUGHES

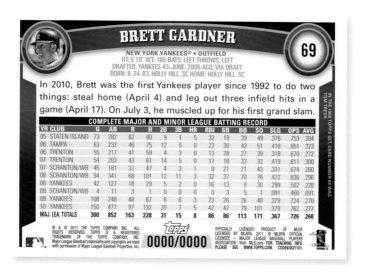

BRETT GARDNER

NEW YORK YANKEES® • OUTFIELD
HT: 5'10" WT: 185 BATS: LEFT THROWS: LEFT
DRAFTED: YANKEES #3–JUNE, 2005 ACQ: VIA DRAFT
BORN: 8-24-83, HOLLY HILL, SC HOME: HOLLY HILL, SC

69

In 2010, Brett was the first Yankees player since 1992 to do two things: steal home (April 4) and leg out three infield hits in a game (April 17). On July 3, he muscled up for his first grand slam.

COMPLETE MAJOR AND MINOR LEAGUE BATTING RECORD														
YR CLUB	G	AB	R	H	2B	3B	HR	RBI	SB	BB	SO	SLG	OPS	AVG
05 STATEN ISLAND	73	282	62	80	9	1	5	32	19	39	49	.376	.753	.284
06 TAMPA	63	232	46	75	12	5	0	22	30	43	51	.418	.851	.323
06 TRENTON	55	217	41	59	4	3	0	13	28	27	39	.318	.670	.272
07 TRENTON	54	203	43	61	14	5	0	17	18	33	32	.419	.811	.300
07 SCRANTON/WB	45	181	37	47	4	3	1	9	21	21	43	.331	.674	.260
08 SCRANTON/WB	94	341	68	101	12	11	3	32	37	70	76	.422	.836	.296
08 YANKEES	42	127	18	29	5	2	0	16	13	8	30	.299	.582	.228
09 SCRANTON/WB	4	11	3	1	0	0	0	0	3	5	1	.091	.466	.091
09 YANKEES	108	248	48	67	8	6	3	23	26	26	40	.379	.724	.270
10 YANKEES	150	477	97	132	20	7	5	47	47	79	101	.379	.762	.277
MAJ. LEA. TOTALS	300	852	163	228	31	15	8	86	86	113	171	.367	.726	.268

IN THE 1988 TOPPS SET, CARD NUMBER 69 WAS TOM FRESH.

BRETT GARDNER   Gardner's game is all about speed: chasing down balls hit to Yankee Stadium's tricky left field, bunting for base hits, stealing bases. *New York Times* baseball analyst Tyler Kepner, describing the sight of Gardner legging out a triple, once wrote that he "whistled around the bases like a cartoon character." Gardy flashed his hustling ways as a walk-on, three-year starter at the College of Charleston, where in 2004 he produced the nation's third-best batting average (.447) and was tied for most hits (122). Drafted by the Yankees a year later, he made his MLB debut in '08 and was the ever-ready left fielder by 2010.

Topps card pictured: 2011 #69. Gardner was also in Topps' 2011 Heritage set (#338), based on the 1962 card design.

BRETT GARDNER

OUTFIELD

NEW YORK YANKEES

NEW YORK YANKEES

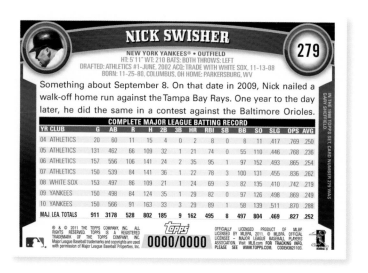

NICK SWISHER

NEW YORK YANKEES® • OUTFIELD
HT: 5'11" WT: 210 BATS: BOTH THROWS: LEFT
DRAFTED: ATHLETICS #1–JUNE, 2002 ACQ: TRADE WITH WHITE SOX, 11-13-08
BORN: 11-25-80, COLUMBUS, OH HOME: PARKERSBURG, WV

279

Something about September 8. On that date in 2009, Nick nailed a walk-off home run against the Tampa Bay Rays. One year to the day later, he did the same in a contest against the Baltimore Orioles.

COMPLETE MAJOR LEAGUE BATTING RECORD

YR CLUB	G	AB	R	H	2B	3B	HR	RBI	SB	BB	SO	SLG	OPS	AVG
04 ATHLETICS	20	60	11	15	4	0	2	8	0	8	11	.417	.769	.250
05 ATHLETICS	131	462	66	109	32	1	21	74	0	55	110	.446	.768	.236
06 ATHLETICS	157	556	106	141	24	2	35	95	1	97	152	.493	.865	.254
07 ATHLETICS	150	539	84	141	36	1	22	78	3	100	131	.455	.836	.262
08 WHITE SOX	153	497	86	109	21	1	24	69	3	82	135	.410	.742	.219
09 YANKEES	150	498	84	124	35	1	29	82	0	97	126	.498	.869	.249
10 YANKEES	150	566	91	163	33	3	29	89	1	58	139	.511	.870	.288
MAJ. LEA. TOTALS	**911**	**3178**	**528**	**802**	**185**	**9**	**162**	**495**	**8**	**497**	**804**	**.469**	**.827**	**.252**

0000/0000

IN THE 1998 TOPPS SET, CARD NUMBER 279 WAS GARY SHEFFIELD.

NICK SWISHER   Every clubhouse needs a fun-loving character, and the Yankees found a productive one when they traded for Swisher before the 2009 season. In his first two years in pinstripes, the ebullient right fielder scored 175 runs, drove in 171, and connected for 58 homers. Fans' online votes sent the switch-hitter to his first All-Star Game in 2010, and he finished the year with a personal-best .288 batting average. Swisher's outsize personality was in full bloom the three times he delivered walk-off hits that season, winning not only the games but also pitcher A. J. Burnett's cream-pie-to-the-face routine, which Swisher ate up with relish.

Topps card pictured: 2011 #279. Swisher's first Topps card (2005 #452) reported that he was named to *Baseball America*'s 2004 Minor League Overall All-Stars Second Team—and that he's the son of former Cubs All-Star catcher Steve Swisher.

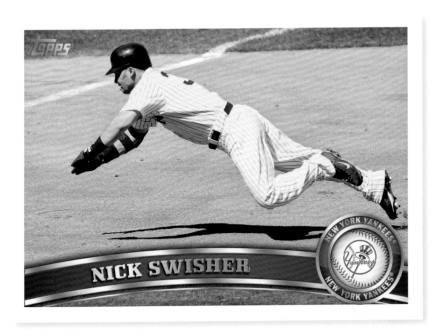

NICK SWISHER

OUTFIELD

NEW YORK YANKEES

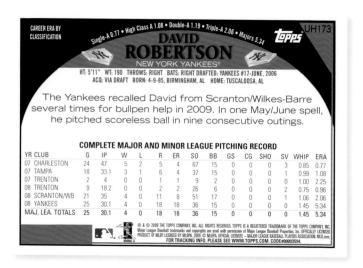

Single-A 0.77 • High Class A 1.08 • Double-A 1.19 • Triple-A 2.06 • Majors 5.34

Topps

UH173

DAVID ROBERTSON

NEW YORK YANKEES®

HT: 5'11" WT: 190 THROWS: RIGHT BATS: RIGHT DRAFTED: YANKEES #17-JUNE, 2006
ACQ: VIA DRAFT BORN: 4-9-85, BIRMINGHAM, AL HOME: TUSCALOOSA, AL

The Yankees recalled David from Scranton/Wilkes-Barre several times for bullpen help in 2009. In one May/June spell, he pitched scoreless ball in nine consecutive outings.

COMPLETE MAJOR AND MINOR LEAGUE PITCHING RECORD

YR CLUB	G	IP	W	L	R	ER	SO	BB	GS	CG	SHO	SV	WHIP	ERA
07 CHARLESTON	24	47	5	2	5	4	67	15	0	0	0	3	0.85	0.77
07 TAMPA	18	33.1	3	1	6	4	37	15	0	0	0	1	0.99	1.08
07 TRENTON	2	4	0	0	1	1	9	2	0	0	0	0	1.00	2.25
08 TRENTON	9	18.2	0	0	2	2	26	6	0	0	0	2	0.75	0.96
08 SCRANTON/WB	21	35	4	0	11	8	51	17	0	0	0	1	1.06	2.06
08 YANKEES	25	30.1	4	0	18	18	36	15	0	0	0	0	1.45	5.34
MAJ. LEA. TOTALS	25	30.1	4	0	18	18	36	15	0	0	0	0	1.45	5.34

DAVID ROBERTSON In 2011, Robertson and his wife, Erin, established a foundation to aid victims of that spring's tornadoes, which devastated his hometown of Tuscaloosa and other parts of Alabama. High Socks for Hope donated $100 for every strikeout the reliever—who wears his uniform socks up high—recorded. The foundation, and the Yankees, rejoiced every time he rung up another, which he did with welcomed frequency. After he debuted with the Yanks in 2008 and helped them win the World Series in '09, Robertson's role out of the bullpen was unclear in 2011 until injuries to other relievers made him closer Mariano Rivera's strikeout-happy, eighth-inning setup man.

Topps card pictured: 2009 Update Target #UH173. Topps honored Robertson's selection to the 2011 AL All-Star team with a "Stitches" relic card (#AS16), featuring a piece of one of his All-Star workout jerseys.

Topps

YANKEES®

P DAVID ROBERTSON

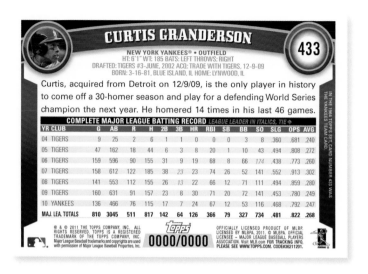

CURTIS GRANDERSON Granderson arrived in New York from Detroit in 2010, following an All-Star season in which he hit 30 home runs, stole 30 bases, and adroitly roamed center field. Whether it was the bigger stage in the Bronx or too-high expectations, his first Yankees season—24 home runs, 12 stolen bases, and a .247 batting average—was deemed disappointing. What a difference a year makes. In 2011, the affable Granderson was an All-Star again and finished the season leading the major leagues in runs (136) and the AL in RBIs (119). Combined with his stellar stats in center, he was a viable MVP candidate.

Topps card pictured: 2011 #433. Series 1 of the 2011 set includes 10 "History of Topps" cards, chronicling such highlights as the first traded set (1972), the reintroduction of Bowman (1989), and the company's move from Brooklyn to Manhattan (1994).

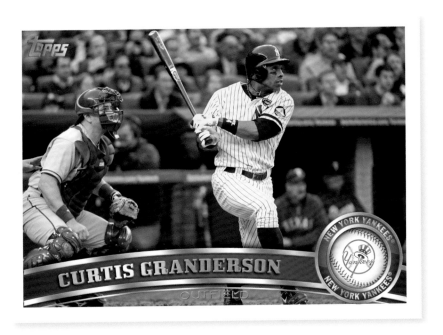

CURTIS GRANDERSON

OUTFIELD

NEW YORK YANKEES

NEW YORK YANKEES

BABE AND MGR. HUGGINS

Miller Huggins was the New York Yankees' manager in 1920. He was the man most responsible for Babe wearing the Yankee pin-stripes that year, for he had convinced the New York owner to buy Ruth. In his last year with Boston in 1919, the slugger had crashed 29 home runs to establish a high for that era. But as a Yankee in 1920, April passed without the Babe hitting a single homer. Just when the front office started getting a little worried about the money that they had shelled out, Ruth started to connect. At the end of the year he had hit 54 home runs. The Babe didn't believe in curfews and this led to frequent quarrels with his manager. Finally Miller Huggins fined Ruth $5000, a record sum at that time. Although there was friction between them at times, Miller's death in 1930 was severely felt by Babe.

©T.C.G. PRTD. IN U.S.A.

MILLER HUGGINS Might Mite—as the 5-foot-6, 140-pound Huggins was nicknamed—turned an above-average career as a base-stealing second baseman into a Hall of Fame career as a manager. After hitting .265 over 13 seasons for the Reds and the Cardinals (for whom he became a player-manager in 1913), Huggins took over the Yankees two years before Babe Ruth arrived in 1920. Known as a no-nonsense disciplinarian who railed against but ultimately forgave the Babe's off-field transgressions, Huggins steered the Yanks—featuring the immortal Murderers' Row that powered the 1927 team, considered one of baseball's greatest ever—to their first three World Series titles.

Topps card pictured: 1962 #137. This card is one of 10 in the '62 set celebrating the life of the Babe.

BABE RUTH SPECIAL

BABE AND MGR. HUGGINS

CASEY STENGEL A good-hitting outfielder for the Brooklyn Dodgers, New York Giants, and three other big league clubs from 1912 to '25, Stengel segued from player to coach to minor league manager, then launched his managerial career in the majors with Brooklyn's bums in 1934. In 1949 he took over an emergent Yankees team that promptly won a yet-unequaled five world championships in a row. The famously talkative Ol' Perfessor won two more championships with the Yanks, managing a pantheon of Hall of Famers, before his own Cooperstown induction in 1966—a year after finishing four seasons as the original helmsman of the lovable Mets.

Topps card pictured: 1960 #227. The photo on Stengel's 1960 card was used again on his 1962 Topps card, when he became manager of the expansion Mets.

CASEY STENGEL
MANAGER • NEW YORK

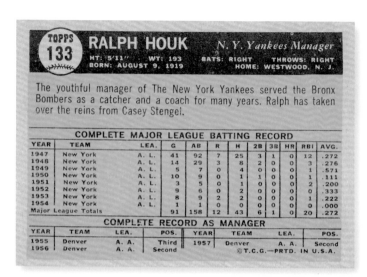

The youthful manager of The New York Yankees served the Bronx Bombers as a catcher and a coach for many years. Ralph has taken over the reins from Casey Stengel.

COMPLETE MAJOR LEAGUE BATTING RECORD

YEAR	TEAM	LEA.	G	AB	R	H	2B	3B	HR	RBI	AVG.
1947	New York	A. L.	41	92	7	25	3	1	0	12	.272
1948	New York	A. L.	14	29	3	8	2	0	0	3	.276
1949	New York	A. L.	5	7	0	4	0	0	0	1	.571
1950	New York	A. L.	10	9	0	1	1	0	0	1	.111
1951	New York	A. L.	3	5	0	1	0	0	0	2	.200
1952	New York	A. L.	9	6	0	2	0	0	0	0	.333
1953	New York	A. L.	8	9	2	2	0	0	0	1	.222
1954	New York	A. L.	1	1	0	0	0	0	0	0	.000
Major League Totals			91	158	12	43	6	1	0	20	.272

COMPLETE RECORD AS MANAGER

YEAR	TEAM	LEA.	POS.	YEAR	TEAM	LEA.	POS.
1955	Denver	A. A.	Third	1957	Denver	A. A.	Second
1956	Denver	A. A.	Second				

©T.C.G.—PRTD. IN U.S.A.

RALPH HOUK   Under the tutelage of Ol' Perfessor Stengel for three years as a coach, Houk inherited the skipper's spot in 1961, winning two straight world championships and the AL pennant in '63. He'd been a catcher in the Yankees' farm system before joining the Army and earning a Silver Star and Purple Heart in World War II. He returned and played sparingly for the Yanks, eventually taking the reins just as Mantle and Maris began their historic home run derby in 1961. After stints as New York's VP and GM, Houk was back in the dugout for eight years, then helmed the Tigers and the Red Sox.

Topps card pictured: 1961 #133. Houk's 1952 Topps card (#200), when he was a catcher for the Yanks, notes that he rose from private to major with the Marine Rangers during World War II.

RALPH HOUK

Mgr.   New York Yankees

BILLY MARTIN Martin proved to be as mercurial as the on-again, off-again manager of the Yankees during their 1970s Bronx Zoo days as he was when he played for the team during its 1950s dynasty days. Not as gifted as his buddies Mantle and Ford, he still contributed to five title teams. After managing the Twins, Tigers, and Rangers, Martin brought his unpredictable brand of "Billy Ball" to the Bronx in 1975, winning a championship in '77. His fiery personality didn't always mix well with owner George Steinbrenner's, leading to five infamous hirings and firings that kept New York players, fans, and media on their toes.

Topps card pictured: 1978 #721. Martin's tempestuous relationship with Yankees owner George Steinbrenner led to Martin's firing during the 1978 season. He was replaced for one game by Dick Howser, then Bob Lemon took the reins for the remainder of the season.

AS PLAYER   AS MANAGER

Yankees

BILLY MARTIN

626 YANKEES TEAM CHECKLIST

Card #	Player	Position	Unif. #
179 ☐	Beattie, Jim	Pitcher	45
582 ☐	Blair, Paul	Outfield	2
335 ☐	Chambliss, Chris	First Base	10
434 ☐	Clay, Ken	Pitcher	43
485 ☐	Dent, Bucky	Shortstop	20
35 ☐	Figueroa, Ed	Pitcher	31
225 ☐	Gossage, Rich	Pitcher	54
500 ☐	Guidry, Ron	Pitcher	49
140 ☐	Gullett, Don	Pitcher	35
670 ☐	Hunter, Jim	Pitcher	29
700 ☐	Jackson, Reggie	Outfield	44
114 ☐	Johnson, Cliff	DH-Catcher	41
558 ☐	Johnstone, Jay	Outfield	27
634 ☐	Lindblad, Paul	Pitcher	36
365 ☐	Lyle, Sparky	Pitcher	28
278 ☐	Messersmith, Andy	Pitcher	47
310 ☐	Munson, Thurman	Catcher	15
460 ☐	Nettles, Graig	Third Base	9
648 ☐	Piniella, Lou	Outfield	14
710 ☐	PROSPECTS FOR 1979		
250 ☐	Randolph, Willie	Second Base	30
60 ☐	Rivers, Mickey	Outfield	17
599 ☐	Spencer, Jim	DH-First Base	12
16 ☐	Stanley, Fred	SS-Third Base	11
387 ☐	Thomasson, Gary	OF-First Base	24
89 ☐	Tidrow, Dick	Pitcher	19
159 ☐	White, Roy	Outfield	6

BOB LEMON As respective Yankees managers, Lemon was ice to Billy Martin's fire. And while the even-tempered Lemon once replaced the tempestuous Martin after a George Steinbrenner firing, Lemon himself was twice replaced because of owner impetuousness. Lemon nurtured his calm as a seven-time All-Star pitcher for the Indians, winning 20-plus games seven seasons and hurling a no-hitter in 1948. He managed in the minors before taking over the Royals in 1970. Lemon famously succeeded Martin in mid-summer 1978, guiding the then third-place Yankees to a tie for first, followed by a historic one-game victory over the Red Sox, and finally to a World Series win versus the Dodgers.

Topps card pictured: 1979 #626. In response to the unsettled nature of the job at the time, Topps issued 1978 Yankees manager cards for both Lemon and Billy Martin—whom Lemon replaced that season after 94 games.

BOB
LEMON

MANAGER

YANKEES

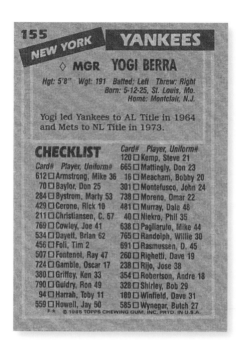

155 NEW YORK YANKEES

◇ MGR **YOGI BERRA**

Hgt: 5'8" Wgt: 191 Batted: Left Threw: Right
Born: 5-12-25, St. Louis, Mo.
Home: Montclair, N.J.

Yogi led Yankees to AL Title in 1964
and Mets to NL Title in 1973.

CHECKLIST

Card#	Player, Uniform#
612☐	Armstrong, Mike 36
70☐	Baylor, Don 25
284☐	Bystrom, Marty 53
429☐	Cerone, Rick 10
211☐	Christiansen, C. 57
769☐	Cowley, Joe 41
534☐	Dayett, Brian 62
456☐	Foli, Tim 2
507☐	Fontenot, Ray 47
724☐	Gamble, Oscar 17
380☐	Griffey, Ken 33
790☐	Guidry, Ron 49
94☐	Harrah, Toby 11
559☐	Howell, Jay 50
120☐	Kemp, Steve 21
665☐	Mattingly, Don 23
16☐	Meacham, Bobby 20
301☐	Montefusco, John 24
738☐	Moreno, Omar 22
481☐	Murray, Dale 48
40☐	Niekro, Phil 35
638☐	Pagliarulo, Mike 44
765☐	Randolph, Willie 30
691☐	Rasmussen, D. 45
260☐	Righetti, Dave 19
238☐	Rijo, Jose 38
354☐	Robertson, Andre 18
328☐	Shirley, Bob 29
180☐	Winfield, Dave 31
585☐	Wynegar, Butch 27

© 1985 TOPPS CHEWING GUM, INC. PRTD. IN U.S.A.

YOGI BERRA In Yogi's first of two tenures as Yankees manager, in 1964, he led his former team to its fifth consecutive pennant, but lost the World Series to the Cardinals in seven games and was one and done. He crossed town to the Mets and served as a coach until 1972, when he took over after the death of skipper Gil Hodges. The Mets amazingly won the '73 pennant, but dropped the Series to Oakland. Yogi was a Yankees coach from 1976 to '83 before taking the wheel once more, steering the '84 Bombers to a third-place finish. He was unceremoniously fired in '85 after starting 6–10.

Topps card pictured: 1985 #155. One of the "Father-Son" cards (#136) in the 1985 set featured former Yankees reliever Bill Kunkel (father of Jeff Kunkel), then an umpire. In fact, he retired before the '85 season, succumbed to cancer that May, and remains the last major leaguer to ump an MLB game.

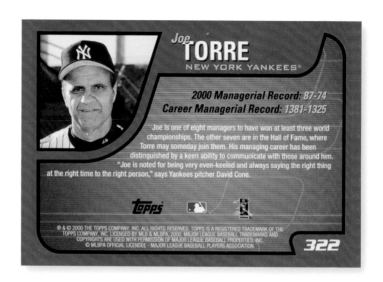

JOE TORRE The news that Joe Torre would replace Buck Showalter as manager of the Yankees in 1996 got a tepid reception around New York. Torre had been an excellent player during the 1960s and '70s, highlighted by the NL MVP Award in 1971 with the Cardinals, yet his managerial skills—with the Mets, Braves, and Cards—were considered dubious. The headline in the *New York Daily News* upon his hiring, "Clueless Joe," reflected little faith in Torre. What he did, though, was lead the team to 12 straight playoffs, 10 division titles, six AL pennants, and four World Series victories, garnering two Manager of the Year Awards in the process (1996 and 1998).

Topps card pictured: 2001 #322. The 2001 Topps set marked the company's 50th anniversary in baseball and included revivals of past subsets, including manager cards, which were last released in 1993.

MANAGER

Joe **TORRE**

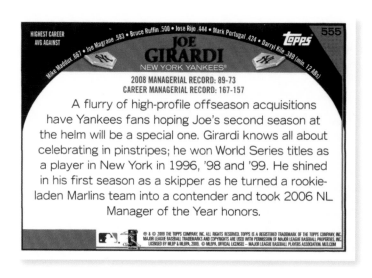

JOE GIRARDI

NEW YORK YANKEES®

2008 MANAGERIAL RECORD: 89-73
CAREER MANAGERIAL RECORD: 167-157

A flurry of high-profile offseason acquisitions have Yankees fans hoping Joe's second season at the helm will be a special one. Girardi knows all about celebrating in pinstripes; he won World Series titles as a player in New York in 1996, '98 and '99. He shined in his first season as a skipper as he turned a rookie-laden Marlins team into a contender and took 2006 NL Manager of the Year honors.

JOE GIRARDI   In 2008, Girardi became manager of a Yankees team that had been a dynasty in the 1990s but hadn't won it all since 2000. He was a catcher on three of predecessor Joe Torre's championship squads and a Yankees coach in 2005, and then helmed the '06 Marlins, earning NL Manager of the Year honors. The Yanks sputtered in Girardi's initial season, missing the playoffs for the first time since 1995 and casting doubts on his leadership. Fears turned to cheers in '09, when the Bombers won the AL pennant, then outlasted the reigning champion Phillies in six games for the franchise's 27th World Series title.

Topps card pictured: 2009 #555. The Yankees skipper was also featured on a 2009 Topps Heritage card (#217), with a cartoon on the back stating, "His smarts punched his ticket to the manager's seat." Smart, indeed, Girardi earned a degree in industrial engineering from Northwestern University.

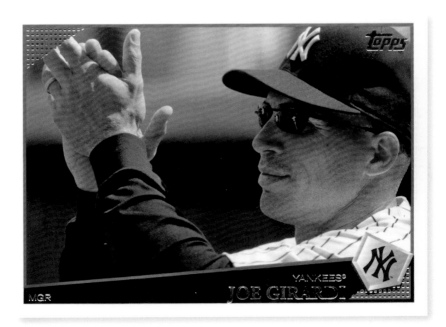

MGR

YANKEES®
JOE GIRARDI

INDEX